THE NEW MERMAIDS

Tamburlaine the Great

Parts I and II

THE NEW MERMAIDS

General Editors
PHILIP BROCKBANK
Professor of English, York University

BRIAN MORRIS
Senior Lecturer in English, York University

Tamburlaine the Great

Parts I and II

—◦◦◦◦◦◦◦◦◦◦—

CHRISTOPHER MARLOWE

Edited by J. W. HARPER

A New Mermaid Dramabook

HILL AND WANG • NEW YORK

A division of Farrar, Straus and Giroux

© *Ernest Benn Limited 1971*
All rights reserved
ISBN (paperback edition): 0-8090-1119-0
ISBN (clothbound edition): 0-8090-9143-7
Library of Congress catalog card number: 72-85834
First American edition, 1973
Printed in the United States of America

1   2   3   4   5   6   7   8   9   0

CONTENTS

ACKNOWLEDGEMENTS

MY CHIEF DEBT is to U. M. Ellis-Fermor's edition of *Tamburlaine the Great, I and II* (London, 1930; revised ed., 1951), Volume II of *The Works and Life of Christopher Marlowe*, general editor R. H. Case.

The editions of Robinson (1826), Dyce (1850 and 1858), Cunningham (1870), Bullen (1885), Havelock Ellis (1887), and C. F. Tucker Brooke (1910) have also been consulted, as well as the modern editions of Irving Ribner (1962), Tatiana A. Wolff (1964), and John D. Jump (1967).

The section on 'The Author' in the Introduction is from T. W. Craik's New Mermaid edition of *The Jew of Malta*.

INTRODUCTION

THE AUTHOR

CHRISTOPHER MARLOWE was born at Canterbury in February 1564, the second of nine children. His family had lived there for several generations, and had been prosperous tradesmen; his father was a shoemaker, his grandfather and great-grandfather tanners. Marlowe's early education is not known, but when nearly fifteen he entered the King's School, Canterbury, and thence he went to Corpus Christi College, Cambridge, two years later. He obtained his B.A. in 1584, and his M.A. in 1587. During these three later years he had frequently been absent from Cambridge, on secret government service (probably as a messenger or as a spy): government intervention was necessary before the university would grant his M.A. On leaving Cambridge he went to London, where *Tamburlaine* was shortly performed by the Lord Admiral's Men. The chronological order of his plays is uncertain. He became not only a celebrated poet and playwright but a notorious freethinker and a reputed militant atheist; at the same time he seems to have continued in the secret service of the government. He was also involved in certain breaches of the peace; in one of these a man was killed (not by Marlowe), and Marlowe was imprisoned for twelve days before being released on bail, and later discharged. In May 1593 he was arrested on suspicion of dangerous religious opinions (Kyd the dramatist, himself in prison for suspected authorship of inflammatory propaganda against immigrants, had informed against him); he was not charged, but was required to report daily to the Privy Council. On 30 May he was stabbed in a tavern at Deptford, by one of three men with whom he had spent the day there, in a quarrel in which (according to their evidence at the inquest) Marlowe was the aggressor. It has been suggested that his death was contrived for political reasons, but there are no good grounds for rejecting the inquest evidence that the quarrel was about the tavern reckoning. His death was described by several contemporary moralists as the fitting end to a scandalous life.　　　T. W. C.

DATE AND SOURCES

The early editions of *Tamburlaine* contain no mention of the author of the play. But though the contemporary allusions which may seem to link Marlowe with the work are not necessarily convincing and the first clear statements of his authorship occur too late to be conclusive, the internal evidence is overwhelming. The style of *Tamburlaine* is so obviously akin to that of Marlowe's other works, so many passages can be seen as echoes and anticipations of other passages in his *oeuvre*, and the character of the hero is so perfect a manifestation of his major preoccupations, that there is no reason to doubt the first clear attribution of the play to Marlowe, Francis Kirkman's in his edition of *Nicomede* (1671).

First printed in 1590, the two parts of the play were probably written some three to four years earlier. A letter written by Philip Gawdy in 1587 describes an accident during a performance by the Lord Admiral's Men which may well have occurred during the execution of the Governor of Babylon in the second part of the play; and Robert Greene's reference to 'daring God out of heaven with that atheist Tamburlaine' in his prefatory epistle to *Perimedes the Blacksmith* (1588) appears to refer to the fifth act of Part Two. The whole play, then, seems to have been written by 1587, the year in which Marlowe left Cambridge, and Part One may even have been the work of an undergraduate. It was certainly the work of someone who had access to a well-stocked library.

Not that Marlowe could have known more than a fraction of the great number of works which had been devoted to the legend of the fourteenth-century conqueror, Timur the Lame, by the 1580s.[1] Timur's amazing series of victories over the proud and the mighty provided a storehouse of examples *de casibus virorum illustrium* for the moralist, and the dissolution of the invincible hero's empire after his death could also be dwelt upon with gloomy relish.[2] Marlowe could hardly have known much of the work of the Byzantine historians, beginning with Michael Ducas' *Historia Byzantina*, written before 1462, and the contributions to the legend by later European historians and moralists overlap to such a degree that it is difficult to identify precisely the works which the dramatist actually used.[3] The books which scholars have generally accepted as having

[1] For a modern biography of Timur and an historian's treatment of the sources see H. Hookham, *Tamburlaine the Conqueror* (London, 1962).

[2] See Roy W. Battenhouse, *Marlowe's 'Tamburlaine': A Study in Renaissance Moral Philosophy* (Nashville, Tenn., 1941), pp. 129–77.

[3] The best discussion of this matter is still U. M. Ellis-Fermor's edition of *Tamburlaine the Great, I and II* (London, 1930; revised ed., 1951). This may be supplemented by E. Seaton, 'Marlowe's Light Reading', *Elizabethan and Jacobean Studies*, ed. Herbert Davis and Helen Gardner (Oxford, 1929), pp. 17–35; and T. Z. Izard, 'The Principal Source for Marlowe's *Tamburlaine*', *Modern Language Notes*, LVIII (1943), 411–17.

contributed directly to the play are Petrus Perondinus' *Magni Tamerlanis Scytharum Imperatoris Vita* (1553) and Pedro Mexia's *Silva de Varia Lection* (1542), which Marlowe probably read in Thomas Fortescue's English translation, *The Forest* (1571), or in George Whetstone's rendering in *The English Mirror* (1586).

Perondinus' picture of Timur is fairly consistent: he presents the hero as a violent barbarian dominated by a will to power. Mexia's version, on the other hand, contains something of the ambiguity which one finds in Marlowe's play. His Timur is both noble and cruel, both a brilliant general and a remorseless tyrant. Marlowe's principal addition to the legend in Part One is Tamburlaine's idealized love for Zenocrate, a theme which he may have found adumbrated in the work of the Byzantine Laonicus Chalcondylas.[4] Nothing of importance in the first part of Marlowe's play lacks support from an historical or a legendary source; what is original is the dramatist's interpretation of his hero.

Part Two is a very different matter. The fact that Marlowe had largely exhausted the details of the Tamburlaine story in Part One has caused many to regard Part Two as an afterthought rather than the completion of a projected ten-act drama and has sometimes prompted the far less valid conclusion that the sequel lacks dramatic unity. Here Marlowe elaborated the theme of the glories of world conquest by turning details from Ortelius' atlas, *Theatrum Orbis Terrarum* (1570), into resounding verse.[5] He presumably found the characters of Sigismund, Callapine, and Orcanes in his earlier source, Whetstone's *English Mirror*; but for the episode of Sigismund's betrayal of Orcanes Marlowe adapted Antonius Bonifinius' account, in his *Rerum Ungaricarum* (1543), of the events preceding the battle of Varna in 1444, thereby changing both the date of the battle and the names of the opposing generals. The subplot concerning Theridamas and Olympia appears to have been suggested by the story of Isabella and Rodomont in Ariosto's *Orlando Furioso* combined with a tale from Belleforest's edition of Sebastian Muenster's *La Cosmographie Universelle* (1575). Tamburlaine's exposition of the art of fortification is a close rendering of a passage in *The Practice of Fortification* by Paul Ive, which, since it was published in 1589, Marlowe seems to have consulted in manuscript.

Instead of being a telescoping of a widely known and fairly coherent legend, Part Two is thus a complex interweaving of a wide variety of sources, several of them having no connection with the

---

[4] A Latin translation of Chalcondylas' Greek was available: *Laonici Chalcondylae Atheniensis, de origine et rebus gestis Turcorum Libri Decem* . . . (Basle, 1556).

[5] See E. Seaton, 'Marlowe's Map', *Essays and Studies*, X (1924), 13–35.

historical Timur; and Marlowe's own original contribution appears in two of the most striking passages in the second part of the play, the death of Zenocrate and Calyphas' cowardice and execution. But even in Part One Marlowe did more than merely copy historical and legendary material. He selected only those details which contributed to his personal conception of his hero. This is most clearly seen in the way in which he actually belies the title of his play: Marlowe's Timur, unlike his historical counterpart, is not lame.

THE PLAY

The prologues to the two parts of *Tamburlaine* are direct addresses to the audience and exist outside the realm of dramatic illusion. The first promises a new form of drama, elevated in tone and free from the jigs and improvisations of professional actors, and the second proudly points to the great success which that new form had had with the first audiences:

> The general welcomes Tamburlaine received,
> When he arrived last upon our stage,
> Hath made our poet pen his second part . . .

Certainly the two parts of *Tamburlaine* were among the most successful plays of the Elizabethan stage. Although no record of the earliest performances survives, Henslowe's diary records numerous productions in 1594–5 and allusions to the play abound even after the turn of the century. And while, with the notable exceptions of Tyrone Guthrie's productions in 1951 and 1956, modern producers have not attempted to recapture that early success, Marlowe's 'tragical discourses' have enjoyed another sort of vogue in our own day. Since the revival of its author's reputation in the late nineteenth century, *Tamburlaine* has been one of the most widely studied of Elizabethan plays. The scholars' commentaries and interpretations have succeeded to the audiences' applause.

Deprived of the possibility of seeing the play in the theatre, the reader must endeavour to recreate it in imagination; and this involves such difficulties as conceiving of a style of acting, the ponderous declamatory mode of the mighty Edward Alleyn, which disappeared from the stage in the course of Shakespeare's lifetime.[6] *Tamburlaine*, of course, cannot escape from time: a twentieth-century mind brings to it forms of knowledge and varieties of reaction

[6] For descriptions of Alleyn's acting see W. A. Armstrong, 'Shakespeare and the Acting of Edward Alleyn', *Shakespeare Survey*, VII (1954), 82–9; and A. J. Gurr, 'Who Strutted and Bellowed', ibid., XVI (1963), 95–102.

which its author could hardly have anticipated. But any serious critical assessment of the work must include an awareness of its great initial success and an acknowledgement of how well its various elements proved to be adapted to the playwright's purpose.

The Goodly Show

The most obvious reason for the success of *Tamburlaine* was the surprise and delight with which Marlowe's novel style was received, a style which has often enough been analysed, praised, and parodied. The majestic march of the blank-verse line with its subtle variations in pace and rhythm; the splendour of the language filled with sonorous place-names and words evoking colour, light, and infinite space; the long, intricately arranged sentences which flow through lines abounding in hyperbole and studded with imagery from classical mythology and the new exploration of the world—Marlowe's 'mighty line' was the source from which the rich variety of Elizabethan dramatic blank verse was to flow. But is Marlowe's style in *Tamburlaine*, as has often been claimed, a revelation of the author himself? Each of the later works reveals significant differences and developments; and though *Tamburlaine* abounds in great lyrical passages, each one is so placed as to achieve a calculated dramatic effect. In its artificiality and in what must be seen, paradoxically, as its severe limitation, the style of *Tamburlaine* exists only as part of a play.

If every character in *Tamburlaine* at every moment of his existence seems to be the victim of a spontaneous overflow of powerful feelings, it is remarkable that the speeches observe the 'rules' of the Renaissance rhetoricians so exactly as to make the play seem an orator's handbook come to life.[7] The characteristic speech, the recurring pattern, in *Tamburlaine* is the 'exhortation', a special type of the 'deliberative oration', and the plot is so arranged as to produce scene after scene in which the characters pursue the rhetorician's primary goal of persuasion, as they urge, exhort, or threaten in an effort to impose their will. *Tamburlaine* is the great drama of primal will, and nearly all of its characters are caught up in the same pattern as the hero, so that nearly all speak alike and the subtlety of characterization to which Shakespeare's drama has accustomed us is scarcely to be found. Though Marlowe can use imagery to differentiate his characters (Bajazeth's speeches, for example, characteristically contain images from the underworld and are full of monsters and darkness, whereas Tamburlaine's images come from the heavens and the classical heroes and soar upward into light), amplification is always

[7] See Donald Peet, 'The Rhetoric of *Tamburlaine*', *ELH*, XXVI (1959), 137–57.

the end in view, and the favourite Elizabethan devices of verbal wit—conceits and puns, repetitions, antitheses and parallelisms—are used only sparingly. But this almost monomaniacal constriction is not due to Marlowe's inability to write in a more varied and subtle style, as his later plays show; rather, it is his means of dealing with the problem of making effective drama out of what has to be, in effect, a 'one-man play'. Having chosen as hero an historical personage whose character seemed as single as his unbroken series of victories, Marlowe had to engage our interest completely in this hero's every action if anything like dramatic suspense was to be maintained. This was not to be a play about the complex relationship of one human being with others but an exploration and exhibition of the true nature of the qualities which the historical Timur seemed to illustrate. Thus each of Tamburlaine's own orations and every speech of his admirers or his defeated adversaries have the same ultimate purpose; and whether we respond to the hero with admiration, awe, or horror, 'there can be little doubt that Marlowe wants us to *marvel* at Tamburlaine and his amazing adventures'.[8]

Such a limited style, ill-adapted to complex characterization or to character development, is likely to produce monotony, and monotony was inherent in the very subject which Marlowe chose: an invincible hero who goes from incredible strength to still more incredible strength; 'a hideous moral spoonerism: Giant the Jack-Killer'.[9] And many critics, even the admiring Swinburne, have found Marlowe a dramatist of monotony, redeemed only by the glories of his poetry. Making exception only for *Edward II*, Havelock Ellis wrote in one of the first volumes of the original Mermaid series that 'Marlowe's dramas are mostly series of scenes held together by the poetic energy of his own dominating personality. He is his own hero, and the sanguinary Scythian utters the deepest secrets of the author's heart.'[10] If so, the attention of the London audiences in the last two decades of the sixteenth century is hard to explain.

However, analysis of the play's construction suggests that the second reason for *Tamburlaine's* popular success was its effectiveness as drama. Marlowe displayed considerable ingenuity in moulding inherently undramatic material into an action which contains its own sort of tension and suspense. The first three acts of Part One are a mounting series of victories against greater and greater odds; but this form of interest having been largely exhausted, the crucially important fourth act introduces complications. Tamburlaine's new

[8] Ibid., p. 151.
[9] C. S. Lewis, *English Literature in the Sixteenth Century* (Oxford, 1954), p. 52.
[10] *Christopher Marlowe* (London, 1887), p. xxxiv.

adversaries, Zenocrate's father and her betrothed, appear with a moral authority which the hero's earlier opponents had lacked. For the first time Tamburlaine is not the underdog in a military sense; and as the Soldan heroically defies the usurper and vows to restore the order which has been violated, we have the first clear indication of the implications of Tamburlaine's heroic 'resolution', his revolting cruelty to his captives and to anyone who opposes his implacable will. Not merely is Zenocrate's plea for her people seemingly brushed aside, but the power-mad despot defies Jove himself; and the ending of the fourth act, with its ridiculous 'course of crowns' and Tamburlaine's assertion of an ambition beyond the bounds of human possibility, leaves the audience with an altogether new sense of Tamburlaine's significance. This man must and will be destroyed, for otherwise there can be no justice in the world.

The fifth act, one of the most complex in Elizabethan drama, begins with the slaughter of the virgins of Damascus. Yet just at the point where Tamburlaine's moral fortunes seem to have reached their nadir, Marlowe inserts the great soliloquy 'What is beauty' (V, ii, 97–127), the play's most brilliant lyrical passage, which suddenly transposes the interest of the drama into a new key and forces us to realize that we have been witnessing not merely a chronicle play about a successful general but a drama of ideas in which the full meaning and implications of heroism, will, and inspiration are being explored. This passage is the idological climax of the play, but it is not the end; for no sooner has the audience shifted its attitude to the hero's character once again than we have the arrival of the enemy army, the suicide of Bajazeth and Zabina, and Zenocrate's portentous lament over their bodies, a traditional *de casibus* speech which prepares for Tamburlaine's seemingly inevitable defeat. But the dilemma of Zenocrate, by now the moral centre of the play, leaves the conclusion still in doubt:

> Now shame and duty, love and fear presents
> A thousand sorrows to my martyred soul:
> Whom should I wish the fatal victory,
> When my poor pleasures are divided thus,
> And racked by duty from my cursed heart?
> My father and my first-betrothed love,
> Must fight against my life and present love:
> Wherein the change I use condemns my faith,
> And makes my deeds infamous through the world.
>
> (V, ii, 319–27)

After this only one conclusion seems possible and right, and it follows with Tamburlaine's lightning victory and his merciful 'league of honour' with the Soldan. But lest the disturbing moral ambivalence which the last two acts' skilful plotting has achieved be swallowed up in general rejoicing, Marlowe concludes the play with a powerful visual symbol: Tamburlaine takes his truce with all the world standing above the dead bodies of Bajazeth and Zabina and the blameless King of Arabia.

Marlowe thus shows considerable skill in manipulating the panoramic structure which his sources naturally imposed; and in the second part of the play, with little historical material left to draw upon, he created a dramatic form of much greater ingenuity. Here the technique of manipulating the audience's expectations for the dramatist's own purposes is clearly present from the beginning. The plot seems to be concerned with the rise of a new and formidable force against Tamburlaine, a force centred in the person of Callapine, who is presented sympathetically in contrast to Tamburlaine's increasing savagery. But parallel to the development of this action is a series of scenes—the death of Zenocrate, Tamburlaine's murder of his effeminate son, the hero's final illness—which reveal the real theme of the play: the inevitable frustration of even the most titanic will by circumstances and mortality. In the action concerning Theridamas' defeat by Olympia Marlowe anticipates the later development of the double plot. Then in the final act comes a surprising reversal, as Tamburlaine effortlessly sweeps aside the just vengeance of his adversaries and at the same time recaptures much of the audience's sympathy, first by proving mortal, and then by a sort of intellectual victory over death. He conquers death by accepting it, by affirming the immortality of his spirit and its continuance on earth in the sons whom he has created. His final defeat proves, unexpectedly, his greatest victory. And yet this part of the play, like its predecessor, ends on an ambivalent note. The speech over the hero's corpse emphasizes his uniqueness, and many of Marlowe's audience must have known as well as the author himself what had come of Tamburlaine's belief in the survival of his spirit in his sons.

As one thus examines the play for the effects which make it good armchair drama, one feels that it must be good theatre too in the form in which Marlowe wrote it; that the 'after-thought' of Part Two is as dramatically effective as the predecessor which called it forth.[11] And yet Granville-Barker disagreed, feeling that *Tamburlaine's* deficiencies in characterization and Marlowe's willingness to sacrifice drama to poetry make the play a poor risk for the modern producer.[12] It is dangerous to disagree with such a sensitive interpreter of

[11] The one modern production is of no help here, since it was based on a drastically abridged text. See *Tamburlaine the Great: An Acting Version Prefaced and Introduced by Tyrone Guthrie and Donald Wolfit* (London, 1951).
[12] H. Granville-Barker, *On Dramatic Method* (London, 1931).

Shakespeare; but perhaps one can clarify the very different way in which Shakespeare's precocious forerunner conceived of drama by some attention to the third obvious explanation of *Tamburlaine's* popular success, the power of the play as spectacle.

For the modern mind the term 'spectacle' is bound up with the spectacular, and certainly *Tamburlaine* seems to contain ample invitations to spectacular display. Its royal personages and exotic locales, its armies and processions and verbal evocations of splendour, might well tempt a modern producer who ignored the simple conditions of the Elizabethan theatre into lavish costumes, massive scenery, elephants, and a great deal of noise. But the word preferred by Marlowe and his contemporaries was 'show', and this word in the Renaissance carried a connotation which it has since lost: a show was a visible means of communicating an intellectual concept. The procession of the Seven Deadly Sins in *Dr Faustus* was a 'goodly show', like Bajazeth in his cage, but its immediate effect upon Faustus is to cause him to ask Mephistophilis to explain its meaning.

Shows, like emblems, were means of communicating moral truth by pictures, and the drama which developed out of the mediaeval mystery cycles and morality plays emphasized the formal emblematic composition of a scene rather than its place in a linear narrative of action. In the evolution of Elizabethan drama Marlowe occupies an earlier place, far closer to mediaeval aims and methods, than Shakespeare, and his plays cannot be approached with the same expectations.[13] Though Marlowe (as has been argued above) can manipulate a linear action for purposes of suspense and tension, and though he shows, in his later plays, some adroitness at psychological analysis, his basic dramatic method is the presentation of a series of emblematic images which, in their suggestion of formal arrangement, communicate their meaning as forcefully to the eye as to the ear. If one objects that the famous slanging match between Zenocrate and Zabina could not possibly have occurred, or that Tamburlaine's speech over his dead wife cannot conceivably represent the actual emotions of such a man in such a situation, or that his turning from his wife's corpse to deliver a lengthy lecture on fortification to his sons does nothing to advance the dramatic action, one is simply refusing to accept Marlowe's conception of the nature of drama. In the confrontation between Zenocrate and Zabina the two women

[13] See D. M. Bevington, *From 'Mankind' to Marlowe* (Cambridge, 1962), and Jocelyn Powell, 'Marlowe's Spectacle', *Tulane Drama Review*, VIII (1964), 195–210. Since the theorizing of Antoine Artaud (see, for example, *Le Théâtre et son double*) and its effect on the modern French theatre it has become widely realized that emblematic drama is simply a special means of producing dramatic experience rather than a primitive version of realism.

cease to exist as realistic characters whose actions are in conformity with anything which we have previously seen or can imagine and become visual emblems of the aspiring mind versus pride of place, symbolic of the off-stage battle which Marlowe's theatre cannot adequately display. Tamburlaine's threnody ('Now walk the angles on the walls of heaven . . .') is not a psychological analysis of grief but a formal, patterned ritual designed to evoke the hero's sense of the cosmic significance of his first defeat and the loss of his inspiration. And similarly, Tamburlaine's excursion into the minutiae of military science when he stands before the burning city which represents his grief presents the essence of his nature in the most revealing dramatic image in the play as, unable to face or to understand the implications of his loss, he finds in the pedantry of his profession the only means to continue action. The passages in *Tamburlaine* which make little sense as narrative sequence exist to make their point as dramatic emblems, each one capable of communicating its intellectual content through appeal to the eye and of occupying its own pageant waggon. *Tamburlaine* is not merely an indulgence in spectacle but a whole series of 'goodly shows'.

The Tragic Glass

But even though emblematic theatre differs in technique from drama which emphasizes linear action, the final result is the same: all of the interacting elements out of which the play is moulded gradually fuse together in the mind of the spectator to create a complete and final response, a response to one's sense of the total 'meaning' of the dramatic spectacle; and the widely differing responses which *Tamburlaine* has aroused have occasioned as much critical controversy as that surrounding any other work of literature. The history of *Tamburlaine* interpretation has been a series of vacillations between extreme positions rather than a sequence of deepening insights. How did the sixteenth-century audience respond to this picture of the Scythian conqueror, and what, apart from writing an effective drama, was Marlowe trying to accomplish? Is *Tamburlaine* really one play in ten acts, or are the two parts so different in effect and intention as to be contradictory? What was the prototype of the hero, and how would a recognition of this prototype have conditioned the audience's expectations? How did Marlowe himself judge his hero, and what attitude, if we can temporarily suspend our preconceptions and prejudices concerning the value and the dangers of the 'aspiring mind', does the play itself enforce upon us?

Both the 'romantic' view of Tamburlaine—the view that he is a perfect symbol of the Renaissance spirit and the spokesman for Marlowe's own aspirations and energies—and the 'orthodox view'—the interpretation which sees the protagonist as a stock figure of evil whose preordained fall is an edifying punishment for sin—spring from attention to only certain elements in Marlowe's presentation at the expense of the drama as a whole.[14] The 'orthodox view' simply cannot explain why Marlowe repeatedly takes pains to soften or divert the condemnation which a conventional mind might be expected to feel for the tyrant. Tamburlaine not merely boasts but, unlike his equally boastful adversaries, accomplishes his vaunts. By the loyalty and reverence of his subordinates and the tributes wrung from his adversaries we are beguiled into viewing the hero as something more than human. Marlowe emphasizes the courage which history revealed in Tamburlaine and adds virtues not found in the sources—his loyalty to his followers, his contempt for wealth, his pure love for Zenocrate—and he is unhistorically made the friend of Christianity and the oppressor of its enemies. His adversaries are for the most part shown to be vicious, and we are reminded that his cruelty to his captives is no worse than theirs would have been had they triumphed over him. His two instances of treachery, to Cosroe and to the Governor of Babylon, are palliated by Cosroe's own usurpation and the Governor's final cowardice. Just when we should be feeling the full horror of the slaughter of the virgins of Damascus our attention is distracted by the fascinating 'What is beauty' soliloquy; and the murder of Calyphas is preceded by a revelation of Tamburlaine's devotion to the sons who have inherited his spirit and is followed by his self-justification, his claim to his familiarly assigned religious role as the Scourge of God. Obviously we are being made to marvel at Tamburlaine rather than to condemn him.

And yet, the 'orthodox' interpretation does describe the general effect of the play as a whole far more adequately than the 'romantic' view of the hero. Marlowe seems to have been as anxious to add to the cruelties of the historical Tamburlaine and to emphasize his savage acts as to justify them. We are spared nothing that the sources reveal and we are given more than any but the strongest stomach can consume without indigestion. The total arc described by Tamburlaine's career does illustrate the traditional *de casibus* movement, for his final 'triumph' over the human condition seems, upon reflection, mere self-delusion, his nature being such that its very essence is negated by death. Thus the promise given in the Prologue to Part Two seems to have been kept in a larger sense, and we are given a

[14] S U. M. Ellis-Fermor, *Christopher Marlowe* (London, 1927) and B e house, op. cit.

second part,
Where death cuts off the progress of his pomp,
And murderous Fates throws all his triumphs down.

The play viewed as a whole seems to have an effect different from the play viewed as a series of individual scenes, which suggests that Marlowe's own judgment on his hero was ambivalent and complex.

A study of the sources available to Marlowe and of the influence which *Tamburlaine* had in its day shows that the puzzled fascination with which Marlowe's contemporaries viewed Tamburlaine's life made such ambivalence natural. The heathen tyrant's barbarous acts and insatiable ambition seemed to qualify his life for inclusion amongst the endless series of moral tales illustrative of the folly of pride and aspiration; yet his invincibility, his failure to fit the approved pattern by falling at the height of his powers, meant that his career could be moralized only by explaining him as the scourge which God periodically sends to punish the wicked, a scourge who, himself evil, will be destroyed when he has served the divine purpose. Accounts of Tamburlaine by the Italian humanists, on the other hand, tended to glorify him as the perfect prince, the symbol of Renaissance *virtù*. Thus Thomas Fortescue, in the work which was probably one of Marlowe's principal sources, at one place describes Tamburlaine's triumphant career in a tone of unqualified admiration and in another chapter lists him among those unjust tyrants who shall not escape the justice of God.[15] And two of the most obvious imitations of *Tamburlaine* use Marlowe's work in diametrically opposed ways. *Alphonsus of Aragon*, generally attributed to Robert Greene, presents an all-conquering, Tamburlaine-like hero in a completely favourable light, eliminating Tamburlaine's atrocities and emphasizing Fortune's favour to the brave. The anonymous *Tragical Reign of Selimus*, however, presents a villain hero, a self-confessed atheist and Machiavellian, whose triumphant career of incredible atrocities is punctuated with hollow-sounding self-justifications. Marlowe's view of Tamburlaine seems by contrast the work of an objective historian whose concern is for the complex truth.

Yet no historian can write without ordering his material, even if he conscientiously tries to do nothing more than reveal the order which he finds in the facts; and *Tamburlaine* as an historical work, as 'more than any other drama the source and original of the Elizabethan history play',[16] suggests an interpretation of events different

---

[15] Thomas Fortescue, *The Forest*, Part I, Chapter 15, and Part II, Chapter 14.
[16] C. F. Tucker Brooke, *The Tudor Drama* (Boston, 1911), p. 302. Cf. Irving Ribner, 'The Idea of History in Marlowe's *Tamburlaine*', *ELH*, XX (1953), 251–65.

from that implied in Marlowe's later effort in this form, *Edward II*.
The view of history as the working-out of God's purposes, and as a
revelation of the moral order underlying Christian ethics, which Hall
and Holinshed inherited from the mediaeval Christian historians
and passed on to the Tudors is not found in *Tamburlaine*. Marlowe
takes over from his sources the explanation of Tamburlaine as the
Scourge of God, but more emphasis is placed on his role as the
favourite of fortune. The scourge is made to fall on the innocent
as well as the guilty, and the tyrant's final defeat is accompanied by
no recognition of sin or evidence of divine retribution. If Marlowe's
interpretation of Tamburlaine's career had a source, it was probably
in the classical historians such as Polybius whose pre-Christian view
of history explained events as solely the product of fortune and
human will, the wills of human beings who are so unchanging in
their essential characteristics as themselves to resemble natural
forces.[17]

   Marlowe's presumed study of Machiavelli has frequently been
cited as an influence on the play; but *Tamburlaine* is, after all, a work
of art rather than of history or political theory, and much of its
inspiration doubtless came from art. The whole of the play springs
from an act of choice and is the elaboration of an emblem, the emblem
which is presented when the shepherd Tamburlaine, inspired by the
presence of Zenocrate, exchanges his shepherd's clothing for a suit
of armour:

> I am a lord, for so my deeds shall prove,
> And yet a shepherd by my parentage:
> But lady, this fair face and heavenly hue
> Must grace his bed that conquers Asia:
> And means to be a terror to the world,
> Measuring the limits of his empery
> By east and west, as Phoebus doth his course:
> Lie here ye weeds that I disdain to wear,
> This complete armour and this curtle-axe
> Are adjuncts more beseeming Tamburlaine.
> And madam, whatsoever you esteem
> Of this success, and loss unvalued,
> Both may invest you empress of the East . . .
>   (Part One, I, ii, 34–46)

There is no need to suppose with Battenhouse[18] that Marlowe's
audience and Marlowe himself would see Tamburlaine here as
betraying the values and ideals of pastoralism; for though the pastoral
mode was one of the great literary conventions of the Renaissance,

[17] Ribner, op. cit., p. 258.
[18] Op. cit., p. 151.

Tamburlaine is here choosing, just as every writer and every man had to choose, between this version of the good life and another which was equally important to Renaissance humanism: the heroic. What is suggested is not the choice of Paris confronted with Juno, Venus, and Pallas Athena, but the equally well-known emblem of Hercules at the crossroads, forced to choose between the path of pleasure and the path of virtue.[19]

For though Tamburlaine's character may contain vestiges of Grendel, Herod, and Giant Blunderbore, and though its conception may owe something to Machiavelli's amoral analysis of *virtù*, the most obvious prototype for Marlowe's protagonist, as Eugene M. Waith has shown,[20] is the figure of Hercules, the favourite Renaissance symbol for the hero of the active life. This figure, which the Tudor dramatists inherited from Sophocles, Euripides, Seneca, and the Italian humanists, was traditionally an ambivalent symbol— egoistic and altruistic, cruel and beneficent, illustrative of both human limitations and divine potentialities—and must have been sufficiently familiar to Elizabethan audiences to give point to Bottom's claim that he 'could play Ercles rarely, or a part to tear a cat in, to make all split'.[21] Hercules, the eloquent patron of eloquence, the boaster who made his boasts good, the demi-god of divine appearance, the gods' scourge against tyrants, was a man of wrath who, in Seneca's treatment, rejoiced in his earthly deeds while never forgetting that he was destined to become a star. He was cruel to women because of his devotion to his *arete*, but Renaissance writers added a capacity for love, as seen in Tasso's Rinaldo who antici- pates the Tamburlaine of Part One, Act IV. The Hercules of tradi- tion finally accepted his agonizing death with calm fortitude, and the dirge with which the second part of *Tamburlaine* concludes could as well have been applied to the Greek hero as to the Scythian. In turning history into art Marlowe created one of the finest examples of one of the great Renaissance modes of art, the image of Heroic Man.

But such a realization by no means exhausts the play or even accounts for it adequately, for Marlowe is obviously engaged not merely in adding an example to a familiar tradition but in exploring the meaning of that tradition's basic idea and making his own individual comment. *Tamburlaine* is an analysis of the meaning of Heroic Man, and that analysis is present from the beginning of Part One to the end of the tenth act. The much discussed question of whether *Tamburlaine* is one play or two has been given too much importance by the assumption that the two possibilities are mutually

[19] Hallett Smith, *Elizabethan Poetry* (Cambridge, Mass., 1952), pp. 293–303.
[20] Eugene M. Waith, *The Herculean Hero* (London, 1962), pp. 60–80.
[21] *A Midsummer-Night's Dream*, I, ii, 25–6.

exclusive. Obviously Part Two was an afterthought in the sense that Marlowe had no way of knowing that the first part would be so well received as to call for a sequel; but it is equally obvious that in writing his play on the hero's youthful triumphs the author was fully aware of his declining years and his death, just as he must have penned Tamburlaine's final triumphant affirmation of the survival of his immortal spirit in his sons with a full knowledge of what those sons had made of the conqueror's empire. Everything that one sees in Part Two is implicit in Part One, for Tamburlaine differed from Hercules in two important respects. First, he was of low birth, so that his path to the 'sweet fruition of an earthly crown' could only be a continual usurpation, and the imagery of the early scenes is full of allusions to the rebels and usurpers of mythology: the Olympians in their rising against the Titans, the Titans in their counter-rebellion against Jove, Phaëton presumptuously guiding the chariot of Apollo. And in justifying his own usurpation by divine precedents and continually claiming the authority of a god, Tamburlaine ignores the other respect in which he differed from Hercules, the fact that he was a mortal man, so that the power of the hero's eloquence is achieved by a wild exaggeration which verges upon the ludicrous.

Since T. S. Eliot first characterized Marlowe's 'most powerful and mature tone' as that of a 'savage comic humour' the question has been much discussed,[22] and it is rendered particularly difficult with respect to *Tamburlaine* by the printer's puzzling preface to the first edition:

> I have (purposely) omitted and left out some fond and frivolous gestures, digressing (and in my poor opinion) far unmeet for the matter, which I thought, might seem more tedious unto the wise, than any way else to be regarded, though (haply) they have been of some vain conceited fondlings greatly gaped at, what times they were showed upon the stage in their graced deformities: nevertheless, now, to be mixtured in print with such matter of worth, it would prove a great disgrace to so honourable and stately a history.

Whether Richard Jones's words mean that the printed text contains the play which Marlowe wrote, uncontaminated by the impromptu jokes which actors had inserted into the performance, or that the printer arbitrarily edited and abridged Marlowe's text, can never

[22] T. S. Eliot, 'Christopher Marlowe', *Selected Essays* (London, 1932), p. 23. Cf. Paul H. Kocher, *Christopher Marlowe* (Chapel Hill, North Carolina, 1946), pp. 267–77; Clifford Leech, 'Marlowe's Humor', *Marlowe: A Collection of Critical Essays* (Twentieth Century Views), ed. Clifford Leech (Englewood Cliffs, New Jersey, 1964); and J. R. Mulryne and Stephen Fender, 'Marlowe and the Comic Distance', *Christopher Marlowe* (Mermaid Critical Commentaries), ed. Brian Morris (London, 1968). pp. 49–64.

be known, though the Prologue to Part One suggests the former explanation and the rather silly fooling of II, iv in the first part seems to illustrate the sort of thing which Jones's words describe.[23] What must be emphasized is that in *Tamburlaine* Marlowe 'could laugh at his hero while sharing that hero's aspiration and anguish'.[24]

The first dramatic image which the play presents is a caricature of the hero's grandiose conception of 'the sweet fruition of an earthly crown': the whining, ineffectual King Mycetes. Tamburlaine's crude jeering at his captives is as little above low farce as the triumphs of Faustus' magic; and at several points in the play soaring passages of lyricism are brought down to earth with a commonplace comment, as when Tamburlaine's most amazing offering of rodomontade to Zenocrate is qualified by 'Techelles, women must be flattered' (Part One, I, ii, 107). The absurd literalism of Tamburlaine's carrying-out of his boasts, as in the famous scene where he drives the captive kings harnessed to his chariot, shows him in a ridiculous light as the prisoner of his own rhetoric. Confronted by such spectacles, one feels as much incredulity as awe and trembles on the verge of that mocking laughter which, in Part Two, momentarily takes over the play as the jibing of the cowardly Calyphas satirizes everything that his father represents:

> Away ye fools, my father needs not me,
> Nor you, in faith, but that you will be thought
> More childish valourous than manly wise:
> If half our camp should sit and sleep with me,
> My father were enough to scare the foe:
> You do dishonour to his majesty,
> To think our helps will do him any good.
>
>   (IV, i, 15–21)

Calyphas is ruthlessly swept aside, but for a moment the spirit of Falstaff has answered Hotspur.

The mighty line itself 'attains its effects', in Eliot's phrase, 'by something not unlike caricature'. When one of the characters in *The Return from Parnassus* vows

> I'll cause the Pleiades to give thee thanks,
> I'll write thy name within the sixteenth sphere;
> I'll make the Antarctic Pole to kiss thy toe,
> And Cynthia to do homage to thy tail . . .

no one can fail to recognize what is being parodied, since the parody is so close to the original. But this is not to claim that *Tamburlaine*

---

[23] Professor Ellis-Fermor thought that numerous actors' jokes remained embedded in the text.
[24] Leech, op. cit., p. 168.

is a comedy, for it is something far more complex. Eliot speaks of 'this style which secures its emphasis by always hesitating on the edge of caricature at the right moment', and what Marlowe presents is not a caricature of the Herculean Hero but a vision of him which shows his outrageousness as clearly as his grandeur. Marlowe's humour is indeed savage, an amoral vision of reality which sees the ultimate absurdity of a world in which brute strength and ferocity prevail, even though the exemplars of these qualities enjoy their triumph only for a moment.

But if humour is one ingredient in Marlowe's critical presentation of Tamburlaine, yet another is 'humour' in Ben Jonson's sense, or what is nowadays called psychology. Tamburlaine is a unique individual with a perfectly clear perception of his own nature and motivations. In the famous passage where he justifies his treachery to Cosroe, he takes his stand on the argument that he must act as he has acted because he is what he is:

> The thirst of reign and sweetness of a crown,
> That caused the eldest son of heavenly Ops,
> To thrust his doting father from his chair,
> And place himself in the empyreal heaven,
> Moved me to manage arms against thy state.
> What better precedent than mighty Jove?
> Nature that framed us of four elements,
> Warring within our breasts for regiment,
> Doth teach us all to have aspiring minds:
> Our souls whose faculties can comprehend
> The wondrous architecture of the world:
> And measure every wandering planet's course,
> Still climbing after knowledge infinite,
> And always moving as the restless spheres,
> Wills us to wear ourselves and never rest,
> Until we reach the ripest fruit of all,
> That perfect bliss and sole felicity,
> The sweet fruition of an earthly crown.
>
> (Part One, II, vii, 12–29)

This astonishing assertion, the very antithesis of traditional Elizabethan conceptions of order and degree, is actually perfectly natural in its dramatic context. Tamburlaine simply displays the normal human habit of generalizing his own nature and impulses into cosmic laws, and his claim to represent a universal norm is implicitly denied by the concluding lines of Part Two where his mourning son emphasizes the dead hero's uniqueness. What Tamburlaine is, in terms of Elizabethan psychology, has been often enough described.[25] He is

[25] See Johnstone Parr, *Tamburlaine's Malady and Other Essays on Astrology in Elizabethan Drama* (Tuscaloosa, Alabama, 1953).

the choleric man in whom one element has gained ascendancy in that war of the 'humours' (choler, melancholy, blood, and phlegm) which, for the thought of Marlowe's day, constituted the process of human life. Tamburlaine's hot and angry temperament, his pale complexion and fiery eyes, his being likened to a blazing meteor, and his victims' hope that his 'hot extremes' may cause him to 'dry up with anger and consume with heat', all prepare us for his physician's diagnosis of his final illness, a passage which stands at the end of the play in balanced opposition to the famous speech just cited:

> I viewed your urine and the hypostasis
> Thick and obscure doth make your danger great,
> Your veins are full of accidental heat,
> Whereby the moisture of your blood is dried,
> The humidum and calor, which some hold
> Is not a parcel of the elements,
> But of a substance more divine and pure,
> Is almost clean extinguished and spent,
> Which being the cause of life imports your death.
>
> (Part Two, V, iii, 82–90)

It is to this that the 'aspiring mind' has attained. The very 'temperament' to which Tamburlaine appeals to justify his aspiration and which enables him to triumph in every contest requiring strength and will is also the cause of his decline and death; and the irony of his great speech on nature lies in his unawareness of the full meaning of mortality.

Tamburlaine's speech is heretical, of course, not because it pictures human nature as composed of warring elements, but because it ignores the traditional view that wisdom is to be found in ordering and controlling such elements so that each provides its proper balance and occupies its proper place. Tamburlaine denies the Aristotelian notion of an immutable principle of natural law, *natura naturans*, an ideal order towards which nature tends and which human nature must strive to mirror, and insists upon the world of flux and strife, the generation, development, and decay of *natura naturata*, as the sole reality. The play itself provides no refutation of such a view, but rather seems to be a demonstration of its consequences, as eloquent a description of the glories of Tamburlaine's achievements as it is vivid in its picture of his savagery and convincing in demonstration of the inevitability of his final fall. And this suggests, as has recently been shown by D. J. Palmer,[26] that the ultimate source of *Tamburlaine*, as of Marlowe's work generally, is Marlowe's naturalism, his intellectual participation in one of the

[26] 'Marlowe's Naturalism', *Christopher Marlowe* (Mermaid Critical Commentaries), ed. Brian Morris (London, 1968), pp. 151–76.

great ideological currents of Renaissance thought, exemplified in
Machiavelli, Montaigne, and Guicciardini, which emphasizes the
discrepancy between the ideal and the empirical actuality and attends
exclusively to matter and (non-spiritual) nature. Marlowe's treatment of nature, writes Palmer, 'is informed by an unusual emphasis
upon the self-sufficiency of purely material cause and effect, in an
order of being apparently subject only to the immediate imperatives
of morally neutral forces'. But *Tamburlaine* does not present a flat
contradiction of orthodox patterns of tragic justice. Rather, for the
traditional scheme of a violation of a moral order followed by divine
retribution and order restored Marlowe substitutes a similar pattern
carried out by purely naturalistic means.[27]

The much debated question of whether Marlowe approves or dis-
approves of Tamburlaine would have received less attention if more
had been paid to the injunction which concludes the Prologue to
Part One:

> View but his picture in this tragic glass,
> And then applaud his fortunes as you please.

Rather than being merely the author's arrogant pretence of indiffer-
ence to the success of his play, these lines may be seen as a serious
statement about art: the claim that moral judgment is secondary to a
sense of truth. A dramatist has no advance control over the moral
views of his audience, and the detritus of citations from mediaeval
and Renaissance moralists with which *Tamburlaine* studies are
cluttered is in a way as irrelevant as praise of Marlowe for antici-
pating Nietzsche. Before a work of literature can convincingly
communicate a moral judgment it must convince us that its author
is not merely engaged in propaganda for an ethical code but has
grasped a pattern actually present in reality, and this is what Marlowe, in embodying the abstract qualities of resolution, ambition,
pride, and cruelty in a completely objective portrait of the choleric
man as hero, has tried to do. Such an intention is as present in Part
One as in the sequel, where Tamburlaine's weakness, merely implicit
before, becomes the major theme. His weakness is that while he can
conquer, he cannot create, for he can work only with the material
forces upon which he relies and is thus ultimately their slave rather
than their master. He cannot renew life in his beloved wife, cannot
create a first-born son in his own image, cannot sustain the ebbing
force of his own superb organism. As a study of power the play thus
anticipates the important distinction suggested by Eric Fromm in
Escape from Freedom between two meanings present in the word
'power': 'domination'—power over men—and 'potency'—the ability

[27] Ibid., pp. 151–2.

to do something, to be able. The two meanings which lie concealed
in one word are actually mutually exclusive, and in *Tamburlaine* the
natural man whose nature devotes itself to universal dominion is
shown, in the course of nature, to be impotent.

Thus, although *Tamburlaine* presents a bold ethic of freedom—
freedom from degree, freedom from fortune, freedom from divine
retribution for sin—which is surprising and exciting in its historical
context,[28] it presents this ethic objectively and analytically, showing
the ultimate slavery of a man free in Tamburlaine's sense to his
limitless ambitions and idealized image of himself. The play does
not present a theology, but, rather, a welter of conflicting opinions
as the various characters attempt to interpret the divine by the light
of their understandings. Tamburlaine's, of course, is the most
powerful voice:

> There is a God full of revenging wrath,
> From whom the thunder and the lightning breaks,
> Whose scourge I am, and Him will I obey.
>
> (Part Two, V, i, 181–3)

Tamburlaine's conception of himself as the Scourge of God seems
to be at bottom a conception of God as might, the unfathomable
natural world itself as the basis of all being and thus the support of
all efficacious action. But, like the speech on nature, this conception
is presented ironically, for the hero is finally obliged to confess that
he has never understood the God to whom he has always appealed.
In the final scene of the play Marlowe, by superlative dramatic
imagination, achieves yet another of those sudden reversals of sympathy with which the play is filled. Tamburlaine's atrocities have
risen to their height; the harnessed kings have been killed, the
Governor of Babylon slaughtered before our eyes, thousands of
innocent people summarily drowned, and the expiring old tyrant
totters above the map of the world, roaring with frustrated ambition
and framed by the corpse of Zenocrate and the son whom we know
will prove ineffectual. And then suddenly we have the dying hero's
last command to his heir:

> Let not thy love exceed thine honour son,
> Nor bar thy mind that magnanimity
> That nobly must admit necessity.

This is, of course, a command to Amyras to assume the role to which
his nature impels him, and thus an appeal to Tamburlaine's old
principles; but the words 'magnanimity' and 'admit' show it to be

[28] See Michael Quinn, 'The Freedom of Tamburlaine', *Modern Language
Quarterly*, XXI (1960), 315–20.

something more. Tamburlaine at last submits to the very force which he had previously regarded himself as controlling, so that his final words, 'Tamburlaine, the scourge of God must die', are a triumph of understanding achieved in the midst of his defeat; and we are left to applaud his fortunes as we please.

High Astounding Terms

'*Tamburlaine the Great*,' Miss Mahood once observed, 'is the only drama I know in which the *death* of the hero constitutes the tragedy'.[29] Perhaps this gives too little weight to Tamburlaine's final moment of self-knowledge and acceptance of his fate, but the point is well taken. We are not dealing here with drama of the same genre as *Hamlet* or *Lear*, and discussion of Marlowe's 'tragical discourses' in the traditional terms of tragedy sheds little light on the play. It has often been pointed out that the relation between Tamburlaine's hybris and his death is casual rather than causal, for Marlowe is writing heroic romance, or creating a history play which lacks what came to be the great central theme of the Elizabethan chronicle play, the unifying of the nation. The actual relation between *Tamburlaine* and what the Greeks and the later Shakespeare have accustomed us to think of as tragedy is that Marlowe here subordinates all the elements of the drama to the attainment of only one of the effects of tragedy, the sublime.

Tamburlaine is the principal example of the sublime in English drama, even if its savagery and its wild humour make its final effect unique. In his description of the sublime Longinus reminds us that 'it is not to persuasion but to ecstasy that passages of extraordinary genius carry the hearer',[30] and a recollection of this distinction suggests the irrelevance of many of the arguments concerning Marlowe's own moral judgment of his hero. We customarily describe *Tamburlaine* as an heroic play by virtue of what it contains; but since the heroic is an attitude of the human will rather than a quality in an object, it would be more precise to see the play as heroic because of what it does. Initially the dramatic spectacle draws the spectator into itself, energizing him with that fierce joy of self-assertion in the face of an irreconcilable world which forces pleasure out of even the most intense pain. But as the full horror of the meaning of heroic freedom is revealed and Tamburlaine looms before us as a titanic force of evil against which no action can possibly countervail, we progressively detach ourselves, from his nature and from something in our own

[29] M. M. Mahood, *Poetry and Humanism* (London, 1950), p. 60.
[30] Longinus, *On the Sublime*, Ch. I. 4. See 'The Sublime and its Vices' in T. R. Henn, *Longinus and English Criticism* (Cambridge, 1934), pp. 10–20.

natures, feeling a sense of wholeness and equilibrium which makes us free. When the hero himself finally attains freedom in the sense of acceptance of necessity, he has reached the same plateau of detachment to which his career has led the spectator, and one is left with the conviction that a comprehensive and impartial view of experience has imparted a wisdom for which there are no words. Despite the barbaric splendour of its spectacle and the soaring flights of its poetry, *Tamburlaine*, in its final effect, is cold.

The style, we are often assured, is the man himself; and Marlowe obviously could not have written *Tamburlaine* without having something, perhaps a great deal, of its protagonist in himself. But in speculating upon the exact relationship between the eponymous hero and the dramatist, it is helpful to recall that Tamburlaine, for all his rhetorical powers, could not have written *Tamburlaine*. The fascination with Marlowe's career as homosexual, atheist, and Machiavellian amoralist has bedevilled Marlowe scholarship and led to too many speculative interpretations of his plays as autobiographical self-confessions. But his life is of unusual fascination and comparatively well documented, and a clearly defined conception of the man does emerge from the welter of fact and rumour. When one compares the image of the man with the plays, however, it is startling to note that Marlowe's two most powerful dramatic climaxes, the deaths of Dr Faustus and of Edward II, are punishments, in some sense merited and inevitable, for the very views and actions which, proudly professed, daily endangered Marlowe's own life. The process of understanding how and why such punishments were both merited and inevitable is equivalent to the process of fully experiencing the plays in which they occur. Surely none of the great rebels—Villon, Melville, Dostoevsky, Baudelaire, or Rimbaud—filled more fully than Marlowe the role of a Prometheus who is his own vulture.

But *Tamburlaine* is not rebellion any more than it is submission. It is a description of the full meaning of rebellion. The final punishment for the aspiring mind is not the fires of Smithfield but disillusionment. If one cannot avoid encountering this play with one's impression of Marlowe in mind, its most striking feature is not the frequently noted savagery and lack of pity, but the absence of self-pity.

NOTE ON THE TEXT

The first edition of *Tamburlaine*, a black letter octavo containing both parts of the play, was published in 1590. Two copies are extant, one in the Huntington Library and one in the Bodleian. Three more octavo editions followed within the next two decades, those of 1593 (O2), and 1597 (O3) being reprints of O1, and that of 1605 and 1606 (O4), in which the two parts were issued separately, being a reprint of O3.

All of the reprints correct some obvious errors in O1 while introducing numerous errors of their own, and no one of them adds anything new which possesses special authority. O1, therefore, must be the copy text.

In this edition the spelling has been modernized. The most obvious misprints have been silently corrected, the abbreviations expanded, and the speech prefixes regularized.

The notes indicate the few instances where mis-lined verse has been realigned. It has occasionally been necessary to supplement the stage directions and to substitute the proper names of characters who are referred to in the entries only descriptively. Omitted speech prefixes have been inserted in square brackets.

The scene headings have been translated from their Latin. The rather inconsistent method of scene division in O1 has been followed, except for the insertion of new scene divisions at II, iv and II, v in Part One and at III, iv in Part Two.

Where a reading from one of the later octavos has been adopted, the fact has been indicated in the notes; but no attempt has been made to indicate all of the substantive variants from O1 found in O2, O3, and O4.

The punctuation of O1 is generally quite intelligible to the modern reader and it has been followed except in instances where it impedes ready understanding. The result is a punctuation which, while inconsistent and often varying from modern practice, is occasionally a suggestive guide to the delivery of the verse.

ABBREVIATIONS

ed.   = editor
ELH   = *Journal of English Literary History*
N.S.   = new series
O1   = black letter octavo (first edition) published in 1590
O2   = octavo of 1593
O3   = octavo of 1597
O4   = octavo of 1605 and 1606
OED   = *The Oxford English Dictionary*
s.d.   = stage direction
s.p.   = speech prefix

FURTHER READING
(Studies not cited in the Introduction)

Brown, John Russell, 'Marlowe and the Actors', *Tulane Drama Review*, VIII (1964), 155–73.

Cole, Douglas, *Suffering and Evil in the Plays of Christopher Marlowe* (Princeton, 1962).

Duthie, G. I., 'The Dramatic Structure of Marlowe's *Tamburlaine the Great*, Parts I and II', *Essays and Studies*, I, N.S. (1948), 101–26.

Gardner, Helen, 'The Second Part of *Tamburlaine the Great*', *Modern Language Review*, XXXVII (1942), 18–24.

Jaquot, Jean, 'La Pensée de Marlowe dans *Tamburlaine the Great*', *Etudes Anglaises*, VI (1953), 322–45.

Leech, Clifford, 'The Structure of *Tamburlaine*', *Tulane Drama Review*, VIII (1964), 32–46.

Lever, Katherine, 'The Image of Man in *Tamburlaine, Part I*', *Philological Quarterly*, XXXV (1956), 421–7.

Levin, Harry, *The Overreacher: A Study of Christopher Marlowe* (Cambridge, Mass., 1952).

Poirier, Michel, *Christopher Marlowe* (London, 1951).

Smith, Hallett, 'Tamburlaine and the Renaissance', *Elizabethan Studies and Other Essays in Honor of George F. Reynolds* (Boulder, Colo., 1945), pp. 126–31.

Steane, J. B., *Marlowe: A Critical Study* (Cambridge, 1964).

Tamburlaine
the Great.

Who, from a Scythian Shepheard
by his rare and woonderfull Conquests
became a most puissant and migh-
'tye Monarque.
And (for his tyranny, and terrour in
Warre) was tearmed,
The Scourge of God.

Deuided into two Tragicall Dis
courses, as they were sundrie times
shewed vpon Stages in the Citie
of London,

By the right honorable the Lord
Admyrall, his seruautes.

Now first, and newlie publifhed.

LONDON.
Printed by Richard Ihones: at the signe
of the Rose and Crowne neere Hol-
borne Bridge, 1590.

TO THE GENTLEMEN READERS: AND OTHERS THAT TAKE PLEASURE IN READING HISTORIES

Gentlemen, and courteous readers whosoever: I have here published in print for your sakes, the two tragical discourses of the Scythian shepherd, Tamburlaine, that became so great a conqueror, and so mighty a monarch: my hope is that they will be now no less acceptable unto you to read after your serious affairs and studies, than they have been (lately) delightful for many of you to see, when the same were showed in London upon stages. I have (purposely) omitted and left out some fond and frivolous gestures, digressing (and in my poor opinion) far unmeet for the matter, which I thought, might seem more tedious unto the wise, than any way else to be regarded, though (haply) they have been of some vain conceited fondlings greatly gaped at, what times they were showed upon the stage in their graced deformities: nevertheless, now, to be mixtured in print with such matter of worth, it would prove a great disgrace to so honourable and stately a history. Great folly were it in me, to commend unto your wisdoms, either the eloquence of the author that writ them, or the worthiness of the matter itself; I therefore leave unto your learned censures, both the one and the other, and myself the poor printer of them unto your most courteous and favourable protection; which if you vouchsafe to accept, you shall evermore bind me to employ what travail and service I can, to the advancing and pleasuring of your excellent degree.

5

10

15

20

25

Yours, most humble at commandment,
R. J., Printer

9 *fond* foolish
13 *fondlings* fools
20 *censures* judgments

8–9 *I . . . gestures.* See Introduction, p. xxi.

3

[DRAMATIS PERSONAE

MYCETES, *King of Persia*
COSROE, *his brother*
CENEUS ⎫
ORTYGIUS ⎪
MEANDER ⎬ *Persian lords*   5
MENAPHON ⎪
THERIDAMAS ⎭
TAMBURLAINE, *a Scythian shepherd*
TECHELLES ⎱ *his followers*
USUMCASANE ⎰   10
BAJAZETH, *Emperor of Turkey*
KING OF ARGIER
KING OF FEZ
KING OF MOROCCO
ALCIDAMUS, *King of Arabia*   15
SOLDAN OF EGYPT
GOVERNOR OF DAMASCUS
AGYDAS ⎱ *Median lords*
MAGNETES ⎰
CAPOLIN, *an Egyptian*   20
A SPY
MESSENGERS, *including* PHILEMUS
BASSOES, LORDS, CITIZENS, MOORS, SOLDIERS, *and* ATTENDANTS

ZENOCRATE, *daughter of the Soldan of Egypt*
ANIPPE, *her maid*   25
ZABINA, *wife of Bajazeth*
EBEA, *her maid*
VIRGINS OF DAMASCUS]

12 *Argier* Algeria
16 *Soldan* Sultan
23 *Bassoes* bashaws

---

19 *Magnetes.* A name which nowhere appears in the text but which has been adopted by editors from the speech prefix 'Mag.' in O1.

5

THE PROLOGUE

From jigging veins of rhyming mother wits,
And such conceits as clownage keeps in pay,
We'll lead you to the stately tent of war,
Where you shall hear the Scythian Tamburlaine
Threatening the world with high astounding terms   5
And scourging kingdoms with his conquering sword.
View but his picture in this tragic glass,
And then applaud his fortunes as you please.

1–3 *From . . . war.* Marlowe's expression of his contempt for the popular
   theatre of the day, with its low comedy, rough metre and rhyme, and
   of his preference for a serious and elevated theme.

TAMBURLAINE THE GREAT

The First Part of the Two Tragical Discourses of Mighty Tamburlaine, the Scythian Shepherd, etc.

Act I, Scene i

[*Enter*] MYCETES, COSROE, MEANDER, THERIDAMAS, ORTYGIUS, [MENAPHON], *with others*

MYCETES
Brother Cosroe, I find myself aggrieved,
Yet insufficient to express the same:
For it requires a great and thundering speech:
Good brother tell the cause unto my lords,
I know you have a better wit than I.   5

COSROE
Unhappy Persia, that in former age
Hast been the seat of mighty conquerors,
That in their prowess and their policies,
Have triumphed over Afric, and the bounds
Of Europe, where the sun dares scarce appear,   10
For freezing meteors and congealed cold:
Now to be ruled and governed by a man,
At whose birthday Cynthia with Saturn joined,
And Jove, the sun and Mercury denied
To shed their influence in his fickle brain,   15
Now Turks and Tartars shake their swords at thee
Meaning to mangle all thy provinces.

MYCETES
Brother, I see your meaning well enough.
And through your planets I perceive you think,

8 *policies* diplomacy
11 *meteors* any atmospheric phenomena
15 *their* ed. (his O1)
19 *through* O3–4 (thorough O1)

13–15 *At . . . brain.* Conjunction of the planets was unfavourable at Mycetes' birth, since the moon and Saturn (changeableness and dullness) predominated and Jupiter, the sun, and Mercury (magnanimity, judiciousness, and wit) were absent.

9

I am not wise enough to be a king,   20
But I refer me to my noblemen,
That know my wit, and can be witnesses:
I might command you to be slain for this,
Meander, might I not?

MEANDER

Not for so small a fault my sovereign lord.   25

MYCETES

I mean it not, but yet I know I might,
Yet live, yea live, Mycetes wills it so:
Meander, thou my faithful counsellor,
Declare the cause of my conceived grief,
Which is, God knows, about that Tamburlaine,   30
That like a fox in midst of harvest time,
Doth play upon my flocks of passengers.
And as I hear, doth mean to pull my plumes,
Therefore 'tis good and meet for to be wise.

MEANDER

Oft have I heard your majesty complain   35
Of Tamburlaine, that sturdy Scythian thief,
That robs your merchants of Persepolis,
Treading by land unto the Western Isles,
And in your confines with his lawless train,
Daily commits incivil outrages,   40
Hoping (misled by dreaming prophecies)
To reign in Asia, and with barbarous arms,
To make himself the monarch of the East:
But ere he march in Asia, or display
His vagrant ensign in the Persian fields,   45
Your grace hath taken order by Theridamas,
Charged with a thousand horse, to apprehend
And bring him captive to your highness' throne.

32 *passengers* travellers, traders
38 *Treading* O1, O3-4 (trading O2)
45 *vagrant ensign* nomadic banner
47 *Charged with* placed in command of

---

36 *Scythian*. Marlowe's atlas, Ortelius' *Theatrum Orbis Terrarum*, located
Scythia on the north shore of the Black Sea, west of Crimea, but the
name was often used to refer generally to a large area in central Asia.
Marlowe seems to have used the terms Scythian and Tartar interchangeably, the Scythians being a branch of the Tartar race.
37 *Persepolis*. The ancient capital of Persia, situated on the river Araxes.
38 *the Western Isles*. Britain.

MYCETES
     Full true thou speak'st, and like thyself my lord
     Whom I may term a Damon for thy love.   50
     Therefore 'tis best, if so it like you all,
     To send my thousand horse incontinent,
     To apprehend that paltry Scythian.
     How like you this, my honourable lords?
     Is it not a kingly resolution?   55
COSROE
     It cannot choose, because it comes from you.
MYCETES
     Then hear thy charge, valiant Theridamas,
     The chiefest captain of Mycetes' host,
     The hope of Persia, and the very legs
     Whereon our state doth lean, as on a staff,   60
     That holds us up, and foils our neighbour foes.
     Thou shalt be leader of this thousand horse,
     Whose foaming gall with rage and high disdain
     Have sworn the death of wicked Tamburlaine.
     Go frowning forth, but come thou smiling home,   65
     As did Sir Paris with the Grecian dame.
     Return with speed, time passeth swift away,
     Our life is frail and we may die today.
THERIDAMAS
     Before the moon renew her borrowed light,
     Doubt not my lord and gracious sovereign,   70
     But Tamburlaine, and that Tartarian rout,
     Shall either perish by our warlike hands,
     Or plead for mercy at your highness' feet.
MYCETES
     Go, stout Theridamas, thy words are swords
     And with thy looks thou conquerest all thy foes: 75
     I long to see thee back return from thence,
     That I may view these milk-white steeds of mine,
     All loaden with the heads of killed men.
     And from their knees, even to their hoofs below,
     Besmeared with blood, that makes a dainty show.   80

52 *incontinent* immediately
56 *choose* be otherwise

---

50 *Damon.* i.e., a perfect friend, since Damon and Pythias provided the
   classic example of friendship.
66 *Grecian dame.* Helen of Troy.
71 *Tartarian.* See note on l. 36 above.

THERIDAMAS
Then now my lord, I humbly take my leave.

[*Exit*]

MYCETES
Theridamas farewell ten thousand times.
Ah, Menaphon, why stayest thou behind,
When other men press forward for renown?
Go Menaphon, go into Scythia,   85
And foot by foot follow Theridamas.

COSROE
Nay, pray you let him stay, a greater [task]
Fits Menaphon, than warring with a thief:
Create him prorex of all Africa,
That he may win the Babylonians' hearts,   90
Which will revolt from Persian government,
Unless they have a wiser king than you.

MYCETES
Unless they have a wiser king than you?
These are his words, Meander set them down!

COSROE
And add this to them, that all Asia   95
Lament to see the folly of their king.

MYCETES
Well here I swear by this my royal seat—

COSROE
You may do well to kiss it then.

MYCETES
—Embossed with silk as best beseems my state,
To be revenged for these contemptuous words.   100
O where is duty and allegiance now?
Fled to the Caspian or the ocean main?
What, shall I call thee brother? No, a foe,
Monster of nature, shame unto thy stock,
That dar'st presume thy sovereign for to mock.   105
Meander come, I am abused Meander.

Exit [MYCETES *with his train*]. COSROE *and* MENAPHON *remain*

MENAPHON
How now my lord, what, mated and amazed
To hear the king thus threaten like himself?

84 *press* ed. (prease O1)   87 *greater* [*task*] ed. (greater O1)
89 *prorex* viceroy *of all* O4 (of O1)
107 *mated* rendered helpless
108 *threaten* ed. (thraten O1)

COSROE
  Ah Menaphon, I pass not for his threats,
  The plot is laid by Persian noblemen,⎤   110
  And captains of the Median garrisons,⎟
  To crown me emperor of Asia,   ⎦
  But this it is that doth excruciate
  The very substance of my vexed soul:
  To see our neighbours that were wont to quake   115
  And tremble at the Persian monarch's name,
  Now sits and laughs our regiment to scorn,
  And that which might resolve me into tears:
  Men from the farthest equinoctial line,
  Have swarmed in troops into the Eastern India: 120
  Lading their ships with gold and precious stones:
  And made their spoils from all our provinces.
MENAPHON
  This should intreat your highness to rejoice,
  Since fortune gives you opportunity,
  To gain the title of a conqueror,   125
  By curing of this maimed empery.
  Afric and Europe bordering on your land,
  And continent to your dominions:
  How easily may you with a mighty host,
  Pass into Graecia, as did Cyrus once,   130
  And cause them to withdraw their forces home,
  Lest you subdue the pride of Christendom.
COSROE
  But Menaphon, what means this trumpet's sound?
MENAPHON
  Behold, my lord, Ortygius and the rest,
  Bringing the crown to make you emperor.   135

        Enter ORTYGIUS *and* CENEUS *bearing a crown, with others*

ORTYGIUS
  Magnificent and mighty Prince Cosroe

109 *pass* care
117 *regiment* rule, authority
118 *resolve* dissolve
126 *empery* empire
128 *continent to* touching, bordering upon
135 s.d. CENEUS ed. (Conerus O1)

---

130 *Cyrus*. The son of Cambises and founder of the Persian empire.

We in the name of other Persian states,
And commons of this mighty monarchy,
Present thee with the imperial diadem.

CENEUS

The warlike soldiers, and the gentlemen,   140
That heretofore have filled Persepolis
With Afric captains, taken in the field,
Whose ransom made them march in coats of gold,
With costly jewels hanging at their ears,
And shining stones upon their lofty crests,   145
Now living idle in the walled towns
Wanting both pay and martial discipline,
Begin in troops to threaten civil war,
And openly exclaim against the king.
Therefore to stay all sudden mutinies,   150
We will invest your highness emperor:
Whereat the soldiers will conceive more joy,
Than did the Macedonians at the spoil
Of great Darius and his wealthy host.

COSROE

Well, since I see the state of Persia droop,   155
And languish in my brother's government:
I willingly receive the imperial crown,
And vow to wear it for my country's good:
In spite of them shall malice my estate.

ORTYGIUS

And in assurance of desired success,   160
We here do crown thee monarch of the East,
Emperor of Asia, and of Persia,
Great lord of Media and Armenia:
Duke of Africa and Albania,
Mesopotamia and of Parthia,   165
East India and the late-discovered isles,
Chief lord of all the wide vast Euxine Sea,
And of the ever-raging Caspian lake:
Long live Cosroe, mighty emperor!

---

137 *states* persons of high estate
159 *malice* show ill will to

153–4 *Macedonians . . . host.* Alexander the Great defeated the Emperor
    Darius of Persia at the battle of Issus in 333 B.C.
166 *late-discovered isles.* One cannot be exactly certain of the reference here,
    but possibly America is meant.

COSROE

    And Jove may never let me longer live,   170
    Than I may seek to gratify your love,
    And cause the soldiers that thus honour me
    To triumph over many provinces;
    By whose desires of discipline in arms,
    I doubt not shortly but to reign sole king,   175
    And with the army of Theridamas,
    Whither we presently will fly, my lords,
    To rest secure against my brother's force.

ORTYGIUS

    We knew, my lord, before we brought the crown,
    Intending your investion so near   180
    The residence of your despised brother,
    The lords would not be too exasperate,
    To injure or suppress your worthy title.
    Or if they would, there are in readiness
    Ten thousand horse to carry you from hence,   185
    In spite of all suspected enemies.

COSROE

    I know it well my lord, and thank you all.

ORTYGIUS

    Sound up the trumpets then, God save the king!

                                 Exeunt

Act I, Scene ii

[*Enter*] TAMBURLAINE *leading* ZENOCRATE, [*with*] TECHELLES,
USUMCASANE, [MAGNETES, AGYDAS *and*] *other Lords and Soldiers*
                loaden with treasure

TAMBURLAINE

    Come lady, let not this appal your thoughts,
    The jewels and the treasure we have ta'en
    Shall be reserved, and you in better state,
    Than if you were arrived in Syria.
    Even in the circle of your father's arms: 5
    The mighty Soldan of Egyptia.

ZENOCRATE

    Ah shepherd, pity my distressed plight

170 *Jove may never* may Jove never
171 *gratify* requite
180 *investion* investiture
182 *lords* ed. (Lord O1) *exasperate* exasperated
188 lineation ed.

(If as thou seem'st, thou art so mean a man),
And seek not to enrich thy followers,
By lawless rapine from a silly maid,   10
Who travelling with these Median lords
To Memphis, from my uncle's country of Media,
Where all my youth I have been governed,
Have passed the army of the mighty Turk:
Bearing his privy signet and his hand: 15
To safe conduct us thorough Africa.

MAGNETES
And since we have arrived in Scythia,
Besides rich presents from the puissant Cham,
We have his highness' letters to command
Aid and assistance if we stand in need.   20

TAMBURLAINE
But now you see these letters and commands
Are countermanded by a greater man:
And through my provinces you must expect
Letters of conduct from my mightiness,
If you intend to keep your treasure safe.   25
But since I love to live at liberty,
As easily may you get the Soldan's crown,
As any prizes out of my precinct.
For they are friends that help to wean my state,
Till men and kingdoms help to strengthen it: 30
And must maintain my life exempt from servitude.
But tell me madam, is your grace betrothed?

ZENOCRATE
I am, my lord, for so you do import.

TAMBURLAINE
I am a lord, for so my deeds shall prove,
And yet a shepherd by my parentage: 35
But lady, this fair face and heavenly hue
Must grace his bed that conquers Asia:
And means to be a terror to the world,

10 *silly* helpless, simple
15 *hand* writing, signature
18 *Cham* Tartar emperor
28 *precinct* province
29 *wean my state* nurture my power

16 *thorough.* 'Through' was often thus spelled and pronounced in Elizabethan verse when the metre demanded a disyllable. There are several
   examples in *Tamburlaine.*

Measuring the limits of his empery
By east and west, as Phoebus doth his course: 40
Lie here ye weeds that I disdain to wear,
This complete armour and this curtle-axe
Are adjuncts more beseeming Tamburlaine.
And madam, whatsoever you esteem
Of this success, and loss unvalued,   45
Both may invest you empress of the East:
And these that seem but silly country swains,
May have the leading of so great an host,
As with their weight shall make the mountains quake,
Even as when windy exhalations,   50
Fighting for passage, tilt within the earth.

TECHELLES
As princely lions when they rouse themselves,
Stretching their paws, and threatening herds of beasts:
So in his armour looketh Tamburlaine:
Methinks I see kings kneeling at his feet,   55
And he with frowning brows and fiery looks,
Spurning their crowns from off their captive heads.

USUMCASANE
And making thee and me Techelles, kings,
That even to death will follow Tamburlaine.

TAMBURLAINE
Nobly resolved, sweet friends and followers,   60
These lords, perhaps, do scorn our estimates
And think we prattle with distempered spirits:
But since they measure our deserts so mean,
That in conceit bear empires on our spears,
Affecting thoughts co-equal with the clouds,   65
They shall be kept our forced followers,
Till with their eyes they view us emperors.

ZENOCRATE
The gods, defenders of the innocent,
Will never prosper your intended drifts,
That thus oppress poor friendless passengers.   70

40 *Phoebus* Apollo, the sun
41 *weeds* garments
45 *success* event, result
45 *unvalued* invaluable
64 *conceit* imagination
65 *Affecting* indulging themselves with
67 *they* O2–4 (thee O1)
69 *drifts* purposes

Therefore at least admit us liberty,
Even as thou hop'st to be eternized,
By living Asia's mighty emperor.

AGYDAS

I hope our lady's treasure and our own,
May serve for ransom to our liberties: 75
Return our mules and empty camels back,
That we may travel into Syria,
Where her betrothed lord Alcidamus,
Expects th'arrival of her highness' person.

MAGNETES

And wheresoever we repose ourselves,   80
We will report but well of Tamburlaine.

TAMBURLAINE

Disdains Zenocrate to live with me?
Or you my lords to be my followers?
Think you I weigh this treasure more than you?
Not all the gold in India's wealthy arms,   85
Shall buy the meanest soldier in my train.
Zenocrate, lovelier than the love of Jove,
Brighter than is the silver Rhodope,
Fairer than whitest snow on Scythian hills,
Thy person is more worth to Tamburlaine,   90
Than the possession of the Persian crown,
Which gracious stars have promised at my birth.
A hundred Tartars shall attend on thee,
Mounted on steeds, swifter than Pegasus.
Thy garments shall be made of Median silk,   95
Enchased with precious jewels of mine own:
More rich and valurous than Zenocrate's:
With milk-white harts upon an ivory sled,
Thou shalt be drawn amidst the frozen poles,
And scale the icy mountains' lofty tops: 100
Which with thy beauty will be soon resolved.
My martial prizes with five hundred men,

73 *living* living to become
81 *but* only
88 *Rhodope* ed. (Rhodolfe O1)
97 *valurous* valuable
101 *resolved* melted

---

88 *Rhodope.* A snow-capped mountain range in Thrace, famous for silver
   mines.
94 *Pegasus.* The mythical winged horse.

Won on the fifty-headed Volga's waves,
Shall all we offer to Zenocrate,
And then myself to fair Zenocrate.   105

TECHELLES
What now? In love?

TAMBURLAINE
Techelles, women must be flattered,
But this is she with whom I am in love.

Enter a Soldier

SOLDIER
News, news!

TAMBURLAINE
How now, what's the matter?   110

SOLDIER
A thousand Persian horsemen are at hand,
Sent from the king to overcome us all.

TAMBURLAINE
How now my lords of Egypt and Zenocrate?
Now must your jewels be restored again:
And I that triumphed so be overcome.   115
How say you lordings, is not this your hope?

AGYDAS
We hope yourself will willingly restore them.

TAMBURLAINE
Such hope, such fortune have the thousand horse.
Soft ye my lords and sweet Zenocrate.
You must be forced from me ere you go: 120
A thousand horsemen? We five hundred foot?
An odds too great for us to stand against:
But are they rich? And is their armour good?

SOLDIER
Their plumed helms are wrought with beaten gold.
Their swords enamelled, and about their necks   125
Hangs massy chains of gold down to the waist,
In every part exceeding brave and rich.

TAMBURLAINE
Then shall we fight courageously with them,
Or look you, I should play the orator?

TECHELLES
No: cowards and faint-hearted runaways,   130
Look for orations when the foe is near.
Our swords shall play the orators for us.

127 *brave* splendid

USUMCASANE
> Come let us meet them at the mountain foot,
> And with a sudden and an hot alarm
> Drive all their horses headlong down the hill.   135

TECHELLES
> Come let us march.

TAMBURLAINE
> Stay Techelles, ask a parley first.

The Soldiers enter

> Open the mails, yet guard the treasure sure,
> Lay out our golden wedges to the view,
> That their reflections may amaze the Persians.   140
> And look we friendly on them when they come:
> But if they offer word or violence,
> We'll fight five hundred men-at-arms to one,
> Before we part with our possession.
> And 'gainst the general we will lift our swords,   145
> And either lanch his greedy thirsting throat,
> Or take him prisoner, and his chains shall serve
> For manacles till he be ransomed home.

TECHELLES
> I hear them come, shall we encounter them?

TAMBURLAINE
> Keep all your standings, and not stir a foot,   150
> Myself will bide the danger of the brunt.

Enter THERIDAMAS *with others*

THERIDAMAS
> Where is this Scythian Tamburlaine?

TAMBURLAINE
> Whom seek'st thou Persian? I am Tamburlaine.

THERIDAMAS
> Tamburlaine?
> A Scythian shepherd, so embellished   155
> With nature's pride, and richest furniture,
> His looks do menace heaven and dare the gods,
> His fiery eyes are fixed upon the earth,
> As if he now devised some stratagem:

138 *mails* packs, baggage
146 *lanch* cut
154 lineation ed.
156 *furniture* equipment

Or meant to pierce Avernus' darksome vaults,   160
To pull the triple-headed dog from hell.

TAMBURLAINE

Noble and mild this Persian seems to be,
If outward habit judge the inward man.

TECHELLES

His deep affections make him passionate.   (a great boast)

TAMBURLAINE

With what a majesty he rears his looks: 165
In thee, thou valiant man of Persia,
I see the folly of thy emperor:
Art thou but captain of a thousand horse,
That by characters graven in thy brows,
And by thy martial face and stout aspect,   170
Deservest to have the leading of an host?
Forsake thy king and do but join with me
And we will triumph over all the world.
I hold the Fates bound fast in iron chains,
And with my hand turn Fortune's wheel about,   175
And sooner shall the sun fall from his sphere,
Than Tamburlaine be slain or overcome.
Draw forth thy sword, thou mighty man-at-arms,
Intending but to raze my charmed skin:
And Jove himself will stretch his hand from heaven,   180
To ward the blow, and shield me safe from harm.
See how he rains down heaps of gold in showers,
As if he meant to give my soldiers pay,
And as a sure and grounded argument,
That I shall be the monarch of the East,   185
He sends this Soldan's daughter rich and brave,
To be my queen and portly emperess.
If thou wilt stay with me, renowned man,
And lead thy thousand horse with my conduct,

164 *affections* feelings
179 *raze* graze
187 *portly* stately
189 *conduct* direction

---

160 *Avernus.* A lake anciently regarded as the entrance to the underworld.
161 *triple-headed dog.* Cerberus, who guarded the entrance to the under-
     world.
174 *Fates.* The three goddesses, Clotho, Lachesis, and Atropos, who
     governed human destiny.
176 *sun . . . sphere.* The sun moved in an orbit about the earth according to
     Ptolemaic astronomy.

Besides thy share of this Egyptian prize,   190
Those thousand horse shall sweat with martial spoil
Of conquered kingdoms, and of cities sacked.
Both we will walk upon the lofty clifts,
And Christian merchants that with Russian stems
Plow up huge furrows in the Caspian Sea,   195
Shall vail to us, as lords of all the lake.
Both we will reign as consuls of the earth,
And mighty kings shall be our senators.
Jove sometime masked in a shepherd's weed,
And by those steps that he hath scaled the heavens,   200
May we become immortal like the gods.
Join with me now in this my mean estate
(I call it mean, because being yet obscure,
The nations far removed admire me not),
And when my name and honour shall be spread,   205
As far as Boreas claps his brazen wings,
Or fair Boötes sends his cheerful light,
Then shalt thou be competitor with me,
And sit with Tamburlaine in all his majesty.

THERIDAMAS
Not Hermes prolocutor to the gods,   210
Could use persuasions more pathetical.

TAMBURLAINE
Nor are Apollo's oracles more true,
Than thou shalt find my vaunts substantial.

TECHELLES
We are his friends, and if the Persian king
Should offer present dukedoms to our state,   215
We think it loss to make exchange for that
We are assured of by our friend's success.

USUMCASANE
And kingdoms at the least we all expect,

193 *clifts* cliffs
196 *vail* lower the topsail in homage
199 *masked . . . weed* disguised himself as a shepherd
200 *that* by which
206–7 *As . . . light* the northern limit of empire
206 *Boreas* the north wind
207 *Boötes* ed. (Botees O1) a northern constellation
208 *competitor* partner
210 *prolocutor* spokesman
211 *pathetical* moving
215 *offer . . . state* offer to make us dukes immediately

Besides the honour in assured conquests:
Where kings shall crouch unto our conquering swords,   220
And hosts of soldiers stand amazed at us,
When with their fearful tongues they shall confess
These are the men that all the world admires.

THERIDAMAS

What strong enchantments tice my yielding soul?
Ah, these resolved noble Scythians!   225
But shall I prove a traitor to my king?

TAMBURLAINE

No, but the trusty friend of Tamburlaine.

THERIDAMAS

Won with thy words, and conquered with thy looks,
I yield myself, my men and horse to thee:
To be partaker of thy good or ill,   230
As long as life maintains Theridamas.

TAMBURLAINE

Theridamas my friend, take here my hand.
Which is as much as if I swore by heaven,
And called the gods to witness of my vow,
Thus shall my heart be still combined with thine,   235
Until our bodies turn to elements:
And both our souls aspire celestial thrones.
Techelles, and Casane, welcome him.

TECHELLES

Welcome renowned Persian to us all.

USUMCASANE

Long may Theridamas remain with us.   240

TAMBURLAINE

These are my friends in whom I more rejoice,
Than doth the King of Persia in his crown:
And by the love of Pylades and Orestes,
Whose statues we adore in Scythia,
Thyself and them shall never part from me,   245
Before I crown you kings in Asia.

222 *fearful* full of fear
224 *tice* entice
235 *still* forever
237 *aspire* aspire to
244 *statues* O3–4 (statutes O1)

---

243 *Pylades and Orestes.* Pylades was the faithful friend of Orestes, helping
him in the murder of his mother and sharing his exile and suffering.

Make much of them gentle Theridamas,
And they will never leave thee till the death.

THERIDAMAS

Nor thee, nor them, thrice noble Tamburlaine
Shall want my heart to be with gladness pierced   250
To do you honour and security.

TAMBURLAINE

A thousand thanks worthy Theridamas:
And now fair madam, and my noble lords,
If you will willingly remain with me,
You shall have honours, as your merits be: 255
Or else you shall be forced with slavery.

AGYDAS

We yield unto thee, happy Tamburlaine.

TAMBURLAINE

For you then madam, I am out of doubt.

ZENOCRATE

I must be pleased perforce, wretched Zenocrate.

Exeunt

Act II, Scene i

[*Enter*] COSROE, MENAPHON, ORTYGIUS, CENEUS, *with other*
Soldiers

COSROE

Thus far are we towards Theridamas,
And valiant Tamburlaine, the man of fame,
The man that in the forehead of his fortune,
Bears figures of renown and miracle:
But tell me, that hast seen him, Menaphon,   5
What stature wields he, and what personage?

MENAPHON

Of stature tall, and straightly fashioned,
Like his desire, lift upwards and divine,
So large of limbs, his joints so strongly knit

249–50 *Nor . . . heart* neither to thee nor to them . . . shall my heart be
found lacking
251 *security* protection
5 *that* thou that
8 *lift* lifted

3–4 *man . . . miracle.* An allusion to the Moslem belief that Allah wrote
every man's fate in signs upon his forehead.

Such breadth of shoulders as might mainly bear   10
Old Atlas' burden; 'twixt his manly pitch,
A pearl more worth, than all the world is placed:
Wherein by curious sovereignty of art,
Are fixed his piercing instruments of sight:
Whose fiery circles bear encompassed   15
A heaven of heavenly bodies in their spheres:
That guides his steps and actions to the throne,
Where honour sits invested royally:
Pale of complexion: wrought in him with passion,
Thirsting with sovereignty, with love of arms.   20
His lofty brows in folds do figure death,
And in their smoothness, amity and life:
About them hangs a knot of amber hair,
Wrapped in curls, as fierce Achilles' was,
On which the breath of heaven delights to play,   25
Making it dance with wanton majesty:
His arms and fingers long and sinewy,
Betokening valour and excess of strength:
In every part proportioned like the man,
Should make the world subdued to Tamburlaine.   30
COSROE
Well hast thou portrayed in thy terms of life,
The face and personage of a wondrous man:
Nature doth strive with Fortune and his stars
To make him famous in accomplished worth:
And well his merits show him to be made   35
His fortune's master, and the king of men,
That could persuade at such a sudden pinch,
With reasons of his valour and his life,
A thousand sworn and overmatching foes:
Then when our powers in points of swords are joined   40
And closed in compass of the killing bullet,

10 *mainly* entirely or strongly
11 *burden* ed. (burthen O1)
12 *pearl* i.e., his head
21 *in folds* when furrowed
26 *wanton* unrestrained
27 *sinewy* ed. (snowy O1)
31 *in thy . . . life* in vivid terms
37 *pinch* critical situation   41 *compass* range

11 *Atlas' burden.* Atlas the Titan bore the heavens upon his shoulders.
15–17 *Whose . . . throne.* The glowing spheres of his eyes reveal a constellation of stars and planets propitious to his gaining the throne.

Though strait the passage and the port be made,
That leads to palace of my brother's life,
Proud is his fortune if we pierce it not.
And when the princely Persian diadem,　　　　45
Shall overweigh his weary witless head,
And fall like mellowed fruit, with shakes of death,
In fair Persia noble Tamburlaine
Shall be my regent and remain as king.

ORTYGIUS

In happy hour we have set the crown　　　　50
Upon your kingly head, that seeks our honour,
In joining with the man, ordained by heaven
To further every action to the best.

CENEUS

He that with shepherds and a little spoil,
Durst in disdain of wrong and tyranny,　　　　55
Defend his freedom 'gainst a monarchy:
What will he do supported by a king?
Leading a troop of gentlemen and lords,
And stuffed with treasure for his highest thoughts?

COSROE

And such shall wait on worthy Tamburlaine.　　　60
Our army will be forty thousand strong,
When Tamburlaine and brave Theridamas
Have met us by the river Araris:
And all conjoined to meet the witless king,
That now is marching near to Parthia,　　　　65
And with unwilling soldiers faintly armed,
To seek revenge on me and Tamburlaine,
To whom sweet Menaphon, direct me straight.

MENAPHON

I will my lord.　　　　　　　　　　*Exeunt*

42 *strait* ed. (straight O1)
42 *port* entrance

42-4 *strait . . . not.* Cosroe compares his brother's body to a besieged
town, his life to the palace, or central and most precious place. This is
an example of the other characters' frequent adoption of imagery and
metaphors which would be appropriate to Tamburlaine himself.
63 *river Araris.* Probably the Armenian Araxes, which flows into the
Caspian Sea.
65 *Parthia.* A kingdom south-east of the Caspian.

Act II, Scene ii

[*Enter*] MYCETES, MEANDER, *with other Lords* **and** *Soldiers*

MYCETES

Come my Meander, let us to this gear,
I tell you true my heart is swoln with wrath,
On this same thievish villain Tamburlaine.
And of that false Cosroe, my traitorous brother.
Would it not grieve a king to be so abused,   5
And have a thousand horsemen ta'en away?
And which is worst to have his diadem
Sought for by such scald knaves as love him not?
I think it would: well then, by heavens I swear,
Aurora shall not peep out of her doors,   10
But I will have Cosroe by the head,
And kill proud Tamburlaine with point of sword.
Tell you the rest, Meander, I have said.

MEANDER

Then having passed Armenian deserts now,
And pitched out tents under the Georgian hills,   15
Whose tops are covered with Tartarian thieves,
That lie in ambush, waiting for a prey:
What should we do but bid them battle straight,
And rid the world of those detested troops?
Lest if we let them linger here a while,   20
They gather strength by power of fresh supplies.
This country swarms with vile outrageous men,
That live by rapine and by lawless spoil,
Fit soldiers for the wicked Tamburlaine.
And he that could with gifts and promises   25
Inveigle him that led a thousand horse,
And make him false his faith unto his king,
Will quickly win such as are like himself.
Therefore cheer up your minds, prepare to fight.
He that can take or slaughter Tamburlaine,   30

1 *gear* business
3–4 *On, of* here used interchangeably
5 *abused* deceived
8 *scald* scurvy, low
10 *Aurora* goddess of the dawn
15 *pitched* O2–4 (pitch O1)
18 *straight* immediately
27 *false* betray

Shall rule the province of Albania.
Who brings that traitor's head Theridamas,
Shall have a government in Media,
Beside the spoil of him and all his train:
But if Cosroe (as our spials say,   35
And as we know) remains with Tamburlaine,
His highness' pleasure is that he should live,
And be reclaimed with princely lenity.

[*Enter a* SPY]

SPY
An hundred horsemen of my company
Scouting abroad upon these champion plains,   40
Have viewed the army of the Scythians,
Which make reports it far exceeds the king's.

MEANDER
Suppose they be in number infinite,
Yet being void of martial discipline,
All running headlong after greedy spoils: 45
And more regarding gain than victory:
Like to the cruel brothers of the earth,
Sprung of the teeth of dragons venomous,
Their careless swords shall lanch their fellows' throats
And make us triumph in their overthrow.   50

MYCETES
Was there such brethren, sweet Meander, say,
That sprung of teeth of dragons venomous?

MEANDER
So poets say, my lord.

MYCETES
And 'tis a pretty toy to be a poet.
Well, well, Meander, thou art deeply read: 55

35 *spials* spies
38 s.d. ed. (O1 omits)
40 *champion plains* stretches of level grassland
49 *lanch* cut
54 *toy* trifling pastime

---

31 *Albania.* In Ortelius' atlas the district lying along the west coast of the
   Caspian.
33 *Media.* The north-eastern part of the Persian empire, south of the
   Caspian.
47-8 *cruel . . . venomous.* Cadmus sowed the earth with dragons' teeth from
   which sprang armed men who began to fight one another. The five
   survivors helped Cadmus to found Thebes.

And having thee, I have a jewel sure:
Go on my lord, and give your charge I say,
Thy wit will make us conquerors today.

MEANDER
Then noble soldiers, to entrap these thieves,
That live confounded in disordered troops,   60
If wealth or riches may prevail with them,
We have our camels laden all with gold:
Which you that be but common soldiers,
Shall fling in every corner of the field:
And while the base-born Tartars take it up,   65
You fighting more for honour than for gold,
Shall massacre those greedy-minded slaves.
And when their scattered army is subdued,
And you march on their slaughtered carcasses,
Share equally the gold that bought their lives,   70
And live like gentlemen in Persia.
Strike up the drum and march courageously,
Fortune herself doth sit upon our crests.

MYCETES
He tells you true, my masters, so he does.
Drums, why sound ye not when Meander speaks?   75

Exeunt

Act II, Scene iii

[*Enter*] COSROE, TAMBURLAINE, THERIDAMAS, TECHELLES,
USUMCASANE, ORTYGIUS, *with others*

COSROE
Now worthy Tamburlaine, have I reposed
In thy approved fortunes all my hope,
What think'st thou man shall come of our attempts?
For even as from assured oracle,
I take thy doom for satisfaction.   5

TAMBURLAINE
And so mistake you not a whit my lord.
For fates and oracles of heaven have sworn,
To royalize the deeds of Tamburlaine:

2 *approved* successfully tried
5 *doom* judgment, opinion
5 *satisfaction* certainty
7 *of* ed. (O1 omits)
8 *royalize* celebrate

And make them blessed that share in his attempts.
And doubt you not, but if you favour me,   10
And let my fortunes and my valour sway
To some direction in your martial deeds,
The world will strive with hosts of men-at-arms
To swarm unto the ensign I support.
The host of Xerxes, which by fame is said   15
To drink the mighty Parthian Araris,
Was but a handful to that we will have.
Our quivering lances shaking in the air,
And bullets like Jove's dreadful thunderbolts,
Enrolled in flames and fiery smouldering mists,   20
Shall threat the gods more than Cyclopian wars,
And with our sun-bright armour as we march,
We'll chase the stars from heaven, and dim their eyes
That stand and muse at our admired arms.

THERIDAMAS
You see my lord, what working words he hath.   25
But when you see his actions top his speech,
Your speech will stay, or so extol his worth,
As I shall be commended and excused
For turning my poor charge to his direction.
And these his two renowned friends my lord,   30
Would make one thrust and strive to be retained
In such a great degree of amity.

TECHELLES
With duty and with amity we yield
Our utmost service to the fair Cosroe.

COSROE
Which I esteem as portion of my crown.   35
Usumcasane and Techelles both,
When she that rules in Rhamnis' golden gates,

11–12 *sway . . . in* have some authority over
25 *working* effective, moving
26 *top* ed (stop O1) exceed
27 *Your . . . stay* you will be at a loss for words
31 *thrust* O1–2 (thirst O4)
33 *and* O4 (O1 omits)

15–16 *The . . . Araris.* The vast army assembled by Xerxes for the invasion
of Greece was said to have drunk rivers dry.
21 *Cyclopian wars.* Marlowe apparently identifies the Cyclops with the
Titans who warred against Jove.
37 *Rhamnis' golden gates.* The temple of Nemesis (Vengeance) at Rhamnus
in Attica.

And makes a passage for all prosperous arms,
Shall make me solely emperor of Asia,
Then shall your meeds and valours be advanced   40
To rooms of honour and nobility.

TAMBURLAINE
Then haste Cosroe to be king alone,
That I with these my friends and all my men,
May triumph in our long-expected fate.
The king your brother is now hard at hand,   45
Meet with the fool, and rid your royal shoulders
Of such a burden as outweighs the sands
And all the craggy rocks of Caspea.

[*Enter a* MESSENGER]

MESSENGER
My lord, we have discovered the enemy
Ready to charge you with a mighty army.   50

COSROE
Come, Tamburlaine, now whet thy winged sword
And lift thy lofty arm into the clouds,
That it may reach the king of Persia's crown,
And set it safe on my victorious head.

TAMBURLAINE
See where it is, the keenest curtle-axe,   55
That e'er made passage thorough Persian arms.
These are the wings shall make it fly as swift,
As doth the lightning: or the breath of heaven,
And kill as sure as it swiftly flies.

COSROE
Thy words assure me of kind success: 60
Go valiant soldier, go before and charge
The fainting army of that foolish king.

TAMBURLAINE
Usumcasane and Techelles come,
We are enough to scare the enemy,
And more than needs to make an emperor.   65

[*Exeunt*]

40 *meeds* merits
41 *rooms* places
47 *burden* ed. (burthen O1)
48 *Caspea* the Caspian Sea   s.d. ed. (O1 omits)
55 *curtle-axe* ed. (cutle-axe O1)
60 *kind* favourable
65 s.d. ed. (O1 omits)

Act II, Scene iv

To the battle, and MYCETES *comes out alone with his crown in his hand, offering to hide it*

MYCETES

    Accursed be he that first invented war,
    They knew not, ah, they knew not simple men,
    How those were hit by pelting cannon shot,
    Stand staggering like a quivering aspen leaf,
    Fearing the force of Boreas' boisterous blasts.   5
    In what a lamentable case were I,
    If nature had not given me wisdom's lore?
    For kings are clouts that every man shoots at,
    Our crown the pin that thousands seek to cleave.
    Therefore in policy I think it good   10
    To hide it close: a goodly stratagem,
    And far from any man that is a fool.
    So shall I not be known, or if I be,
    They cannot take away my crown from me.
    Here will I hide it in this simple hole.   15

Enter TAMBURLAINE

TAMBURLAINE

    What, fearful coward, straggling from the camp
    When kings themselves are present in the field?

MYCETES

    Thou liest.

TAMBURLAINE

    Base villain, dar'st thou give the lie?

MYCETES

    Away, I am the king: go, touch me not: 20
    Thou break'st the law of arms unless thou kneel,
    And cry me 'Mercy, noble king!'

TAMBURLAINE

    Are you the witty king of Persia?

    [Scene iv] ed. (O1 omits)
      s.d. *offering* endeavouring
    3 *those were* those who were
    5 *Boreas* the north wind
    8 *clouts* the clout is the central mark of the target
    9 *pin* the nail holding the clout in place
    11 *close* secretly
    19 *give the lie* accuse a person of lying
    23 *witty* wise

MYCETES
　Ay, marry, am I: have you any suit to me?
TAMBURLAINE
　I would entreat you to speak but three wise words.　　25
MYCETES
　So I can when I see my time.
TAMBURLAINE
　Is this your crown?
MYCETES
　Ay, didst thou ever see a fairer?
TAMBURLAINE
　You will not sell it, will ye?
MYCETES
　Such another word, and I will have thee executed.　　30
　Come give it me.
TAMBURLAINE
　No, I took it prisoner.
MYCETES
　You lie, I gave it you.
TAMBURLAINE
　Then 'tis mine.
MYCETES
　No, I mean, I let you keep it.　　35
TAMBURLAINE
　Well, I mean you shall have it again.
　Here take it for a while, I lend it thee,
　Till I may see thee hemmed with armed men.
　Then shalt thou see me pull it from thy head:
　Thou art no match for mighty Tamburlaine.　　40
　　　　　　　　　　　　　　　　　[Exit]

MYCETES
　O gods, is this Tamburlaine the thief?
　I marvel much he stole it not away.
　　　　　Sound trumpets to the battle, and he runs in

Act II, Scene v

[Enter] COSROE, TAMBURLAINE, THERIDAMAS, MENAPHON, MEANDER, ORTYGIUS, TECHELLES, USUMCASANE, with others

TAMBURLAINE
　Hold thee Cosroe, wear two imperial crowns.

40 s.d. ed. (O1 omits)
　　[Scene v] ed. (O1 omits)

Think thee invested now as royally,
Even by the mighty hand of Tamburlaine,
As if as many kings as could encompass thee,
With greatest pomp had crowned thee emperor.   5
COSROE
So do I, thrice renowned man-at-arms,
And none shall keep the crown but Tamburlaine:
Thee do I make my regent of Persia
And general lieutenant of my armies.
Meander, you that were our brother's guide,   10
And chiefest counsellor in all his acts,
Since he is yielded to the stroke of war,
On your submission we with thanks excuse,
And give you equal place in our affairs.
MEANDER
Most happy emperor, in humblest terms   15
I vow my service to your majesty,
With utmost virtue of my faith and duty.
COSROE
Thanks good Meander, then Cosroe reign
And govern Persia in her former pomp:
Now send embassage to thy neighbour kings,   20
And let them know the Persian king is changed:
From one that knew not what a king should do,
To one that can command what 'longs thereto:
And now we will to fair Persepolis,
With twenty thousand expert soldiers.   25
The lords and captains of my brother's camp,
With little slaughter take Meander's course,
And gladly yield them to my gracious rule:
Ortygius and Menaphon, my trusty friends,
Now will I gratify your former good,   30
And grace your calling with a greater sway.
ORTYGIUS
And as we ever aimed at your behoof,
And sought your state all honour it deserved,

20 *embassage* ed. (ambassage O1)
23 *'longs* belongs
30 *gratify . . . good* repay your service
31 *grace . . . sway* give you a more authoritative position
32 *aimed* O3–4 (and O1)
32 *behoof* profit
33 *sought your state* sought for your position

So will we with our powers and our lives,
Endeavour to preserve and prosper it.   35
COSROE
   I will not thank thee, sweet Ortygius,
Better replies shall prove my purposes.
And now Lord Tamburlaine, my brother's camp
I leave to thee, and to Theridamas,
To follow me to fair Persepolis.   40
Then will we march to all those Indian mines,
My witless brother to the Christians lost:
And ransom them with fame and usury.
And till thou overtake me Tamburlaine,
(Staying to order all the scattered troops),   45
Farewell lord regent, and his happy friends,
I long to sit upon my brother's throne.
MENAPHON
   Your majesty shall shortly have your wish,
And ride in triumph through Persepolis.

                Exeunt [all except] TAMBURLAINE, TECHELLES,
                        THERIDAMAS, [*and*] USUMCASANE

TAMBURLAINE
   And ride in triumph through Persepolis?   50
Is it not brave to be a king, Techelles?
Usumcasane and Theridamas,
Is it not passing brave to be a king,
And ride in triumph through Persepolis?
TECHELLES
   O, my lord, 'tis sweet and full of pomp.   55
USUMCASANE
   To be a king, is half to be a god.
THERIDAMAS
   A god is not so glorious as a king:
I think the pleasure they enjoy in heaven
Cannot compare with kingly joys in earth.
To wear a crown enchased with pearl and gold,   60
Whose virtues carry with it life and death,
To ask and have: command, and be obeyed:
When looks breed love, with looks to gain the prize.
Such power attractive shines in princes' eyes.

37 *Better replies* i.e., actions
43 *with . . . usury* to our glory and advantage
51 *brave* wonderful
53 *passing* exceedingly
61 *virtues* powers

TAMBURLAINE

Why say Theridamas, wilt thou be a king?   65

THERIDAMAS

Nay, though I praise it, I can live without it.

TAMBURLAINE

What says my other friends, will you be kings?

TECHELLES

Ay, if I could, with all my heart my lord.

TAMBURLAINE

Why, that's well said Techelles, so would I,

And so would you my masters, would you not?   70

USUMCASANE

What then my lord?

TAMBURLAINE

Why then Casane shall we wish for ought

The world affords in greatest novelty,

And rest attemptless, faint and destitute?

Methinks we should not, I am strongly moved,   75

That if I should desire the Persian crown,

I could attain it with a wondrous ease,

And would not all our soldiers soon consent,

If we should aim at such a dignity?

THERIDAMAS

I know they would with our persuasions.   80

TAMBURLAINE

Why then Theridamas, I'll first assay,

To get the Persian kingdom to myself:

Then thou for Parthia, they for Scythia and Media.

And if I prosper, all shall be as sure

As if the Turk, the Pope, Afric and Greece,   85

Came creeping to us with their crowns apace.

TECHELLES

Then shall we send to this triumphing king,

And bid him battle for his novel crown?

USUMCASANE

Nay quickly then, before his room be hot.

TAMBURLAINE

'Twill prove a pretty jest, in faith, my friends.   90

73 *in . . . novelty* no matter how new and rare
75 *moved* inwardly convinced
88 *novel* newly gained
89 *before . . . hot* before he is comfortable in his new position

THERIDAMAS
   A jest to charge on twenty thousand men?
   I judge the purchase more important far.
TAMBURLAINE
   Judge by thyself Theridamas, not me,
   For presently Techelles here shall haste,
   And bid him battle ere he pass too far,   95
   And lose more labour than the gain will quite.
   Then shalt thou see the Scythian Tamburlaine,
   Make but a jest to win the Persian crown.
   Techelles, take a thousand horse with thee,
   And bid him turn his back to war with us,   100
   That only made him king to make us sport.
   We will not steal upon him cowardly,
   But give him warning and more warriors.
   Haste thee Techelles, we will follow thee.
   What saith Theridamas?
THERIDAMAS   Go on, for me.   105

                                 Exeunt

Act II, Scene vi

[*Enter*] COSROE, MEANDER, ORTYGIUS, MENAPHON, *with other*
Soldiers

COSROE
   What means this devilish shepherd to aspire
   With such a giantly presumption,
   To cast up hills against the face of heaven:
   And dare the force of angry Jupiter?
   But as he thrust them underneath the hills,   5
   And pressed out fire from their burning jaws:
   So will I send this monstrous slave to hell,
   Where flames shall ever feed upon his soul.
MEANDER
   Some powers divine, or else infernal, mixed

  92 *purchase* undertaking
  94 *presently* immediately
  96 *quite* requite
 105 *for me* as far as I am concerned
     [Scene vi] ed. (O1 omits)
   3 *cast . . . heaven* i.e., as did the Titans who warred against Jove

---

  5 *them.* i.e., the Titans. Recalling Enceladus' imprisonment beneath
   Mount Aetna, Marlowe imagines all the defeated Titans as imprisoned
   under mountains.

Their angry seeds at his conception: 10
For he was never sprung of human race,
Since with the spirit of his fearful pride,
He dares so doubtlessly resolve of rule,
And by profession be ambitious.

ORTYGIUS
What god or fiend, or spirit of the earth,   15
Or monster turned into a manly shape,
Or of what mould or mettle he be made,
What star or state soever govern him,
Let us put on our meet encountering minds,
And in detesting such a devilish thief,   20
In love of honour and defence of right,
Be armed against the hate of such a foe,
Whether from earth, or hell, or heaven he grow.

COSROE
Nobly resolved, my good Ortygius.
And since we all have sucked one wholesome air   25
And with the same proportion of elements
Resolve, I hope we are resembled,
Vowing our loves to equal death and life.
Let's cheer our soldiers to encounter him,
That grievous image of ingratitude: 30
That fiery thirster after sovereignty:
And burn him in the fury of that flame,
That none can quench but blood and empery.
Resolve my lords and loving soldiers now,
To save your king and country from decay: 35
Then strike up drum, and all the stars that make
The loathsome circle of my dated life,
Direct my weapon to his barbarous heart,
That thus opposeth him against the gods,
And scorns the powers that govern Persia.   40
                                        [*Exeunt*]

13 *doubtlessly* without doubt or hesitation
13 *resolve of* determine to
14 *by profession* openly
19 *Let . . . minds* let us put ourselves in a proper frame of mind to
      meet the challenge
26–7 *And . . . Resolve* and will decompose into the same elements
30 *ingratitude* ed. (ingratude O1)
37 *dated* limited, transitory
40 s.d. ed. (O1 omits)

Act II, Scene vii

Enter to the battle, and after the battle, enter COSROE *wounded,*
THERIDAMAS, TAMBURLAINE, TECHELLES, USUMCASANE, *with others*

COSROE
　　Barbarous and bloody Tamburlaine,
　　Thus to deprive me of my crown and life!
　　Treacherous and false Theridamas,
　　Even at the morning of my happy state,
　　Scarce being seated in my royal throne,　　　　　　5
　　To work my downfall and untimely end!
　　An uncouth pain torments my grieved soul,
　　And death arrests the organ of my voice,
　　Who entering at the breach thy sword hath made,
　　Sacks every vein and artier of my heart,　　　　　10
　　Bloody and insatiate Tamburlaine!

TAMBURLAINE
　　The thirst of reign and sweetness of a crown,
　　That caused the eldest son of heavenly Ops,
　　To thrust his doting father from his chair,
　　And place himself in the empyreal heaven,　　　　15
　　Moved me to manage arms against thy state.
　　What better precedent than mighty Jove?
　　Nature that framed us of four elements,
　　Warring within our breasts for regiment,
　　Doth teach us all to have aspiring minds:
　　Our souls whose faculties can comprehend　　　　20
　　The wondrous architecture of the world:
　　And measure every wandering planet's course,
　　Still climbing after knowledge infinite,
　　And always moving as the restless spheres,
　　Wills us to wear ourselves and never rest,　　　　25
　　Until we reach the ripest fruit of all,

　　[Scene vii] ed. (O1 omits)
　7 *uncouth* strange, novel
　10 *artier* artery
　15 *empyreal heaven* empyrean, i.e., the outermost sphere of the
　　　universe
　18 *four elements* i.e., the earth, water, air, and fire of ancient physiology
　19 *regiment* rule

---

13 *eldest . . . Ops.* Jupiter, son of Saturn.
25 *restless spheres.* The eternally revolving hollow globes that were believed
　　to carry the planets and the stars around the earth.

That perfect bliss and sole felicity,
The sweet fruition of an earthly crown.

THERIDAMAS
And that made me to join with Tamburlaine,   30
For he is gross and like the massy earth
That moves not upwards, nor by princely deeds
Doth mean to soar above the highest sort.

TECHELLES
And that made us, the friends of Tamburlaine,
To lift our swords against the Persian king.   35

USUMCASANE
For as when Jove did thrust old Saturn down,
Neptune and Dis gained each of them a crown:
So do we hope to reign in Asia,
If Tamburlaine be placed in Persia.

COSROE
The strangest men that ever nature made,   40
I know not how to take their tyrannies.
My bloodless body waxeth chill and cold,
And with my blood my life slides through my wound.
My soul begins to take her flight to hell,
And summons all my senses to depart: 45
The heat and moisture which did feed each other,
For want of nourishment to feed them both,
Is dry and cold, and now doth ghastly death
With greedy talents gripe my bleeding heart,
And like a harpy tires on my life.   50
Theridamas and Tamburlaine, I die,
And fearful vengeance light upon you both.

[*Dies.* TAMBURLAINE] *takes the crown and puts it on*

TAMBURLAINE
Not all the curses which the Furies breathe,

49 *talents* talons
50 *harpy* O2 (Harpyr O1, O3; Harper O4) monstrous bird of prey
    with a woman's face
52 s.d. [*Dies.* TAMBURLAINE] ed. (He O1)
53 *Furies* the avenging deities of classical mythology

---

37 *Neptune . . . crown.* Neptune the sea and Dis the underworld.
46–8 *The heat . . . cold.* 'Blood, the element which combines the properties
    of moisture and heat, being removed, the balance of the "temperament"
    or constitution is destroyed and only the properties of cold and dryness,
    those of the melancholy humour in the constitution of man, and of the
    earth in the material universe, remain' (Ellis-Fermor).

Shall make me leave so rich a prize as this:
Theridamas, Techelles, and the rest,   55
Who think you now is king of Persia?

ALL

Tamburlaine! Tamburlaine!

TAMBURLAINE

Though Mars himself the angry god of arms,
And all the earthly potentates conspire,
To dispossess me of this diadem: 60
Yet will I wear it in despite of them,
As great commander of this eastern world,
If you but say that Tamburlaine shall reign.

ALL

Long live Tamburlaine and reign in Asia!

TAMBURLAINE

So now it is more surer on my head,   65
Than if the gods had held a parliament:
And all pronounced me king of Persia.   [*Exeunt*]

Act III, Scene i

[*Enter*] BAJAZETH, *the* KINGS OF FEZ, MOROCCO *and* ARGIER,
     [BASSOES], *with others, in great pomp*

BAJAZETH

Great kings of Barbary, and my portly bassoes,
We hear, the Tartars and the eastern thieves
Under the conduct of one Tamburlaine,
Presume a bickering with your emperor:
And thinks to rouse us from our dreadful siege   5
Of the famous Grecian Constantinople.
You know our army is invincible:
As many circumcised Turks we have,
And warlike bands of Christians renied,
As hath the ocean or the Terrene sea   10
Small drops of water, when the moon begins
To join in one her semi-circled horns:
Yet would we not be braved with foreign power,

67 s.d. ed. (O1 omits)
 9 *renied* apostate
11–12 *moon . . . horns* i.e., when the moon is full and the tides high

---

 1 *Barbary*. The north coast of Africa.
10 *Terrene sea*. The Mediterranean.

Nor raise our siege before the Grecians yield,
Or breathless lie before the city walls.   15

KING OF FEZ

Renowned emperor, and mighty general,
What if you sent the bassoes of your guard,
To charge him to remain in Asia,
Or else to threaten death and deadly arms,
As from the mouth of mighty Bajazeth?   20

BAJAZETH

Hie thee my basso fast to Persia,
Tell him thy lord the Turkish emperor,
Dread lord of Afric, Europe and Asia,
Great king and conqueror of Graecia,
The ocean, Terrene, and the coal-black sea,   25
The high and highest monarch of the world,
Wills and commands (for say not I entreat)
Not once to set his foot in Africa,
Or spread his colours in Graecia,
Lest he incur the fury of my wrath.   30
Tell him, I am content to take a truce,
Because I hear he bears a valiant mind.
But if presuming on his silly power,
He be so mad to manage arms with me,
Then stay thou with him, say I bid thee so.   35
And if before the sun have measured heaven
With triple circuit thou regreet us not,
We mean to take his morning's next arise
For messenger he will not be reclaimed,
And mean to fetch thee in despite of him.   40

BASSO

Most great and puissant monarch of the earth,
Your basso will accomplish your behest:
And show your pleasure to the Persian,
As fits the legate of the stately Turk.

KING OF ARGIER

They say he is the king of Persia.   45
But if he dare attempt to stir your siege,
'Twere requisite he should be ten times more,
For all flesh quakes at your magnificence.

BAJAZETH

True, Argier, and tremble at my looks.

33 *silly* weak, unskilled
39 *reclaimed* reformed, restrained

KING OF MOROCCO
    The spring is hindered by your smothering host,   50
    For neither rain can fall upon the earth,
    Nor sun reflex his virtuous beams thereon.
    The ground is mantled with such multitudes.

BAJAZETH
    All this is true as holy Mahomet,
    And all the trees are blasted with our breaths.   55

KING OF FEZ
    What thinks your greatness best to be achieved
    In pursuit of the city's overthrow?

BAJAZETH
    I will the captive pioners of Argier,
    Cut off the water that by leaden pipes
    Runs to the city from the mountain Carnon,   60
    Two thousand horse shall forage up and down,
    That no relief or succour come by land.
    And all the seas my galleys countermand.
    Then shall our footmen lie within the trench,
    And with their cannons mouthed like Orcus' gulf   65
    Batter the walls, and we will enter in:
    And thus the Grecians shall be conquered.   *Exeunt*

Act III, Scene ii

[*Enter*] AGYDAS, ZENOCRATE, ANIPPE, *with others*

[AGYDAS]
    Madam Zenocrate, may I presume
    To know the cause of these unquiet fits:
    That work such trouble to your wonted rest?
    'Tis more than pity such a heavenly face
    Should by heart's sorrow wax so wan and pale,   5
    When your offensive rape by Tamburlaine
    (Which of your whole displeasures should be most),
    Hath seemed to be digested long ago.

52 *reflex* cast
58 *pioners* advance guard of trench-diggers
63 *countermand* control
 1 s.p. ed. (O1 omits)
 6 *rape* seizure

---

 65 *Orcus' gulf.* The entrance to hell. Orcus was one of several names for
Hades.

ZENOCRATE

    Although it be digested long ago,
    As his exceeding favours have deserved,   10
    And might content the Queen of Heaven as well
    As it hath changed my first conceived disdain;
    Yet, since, a farther passion feeds my thoughts,
    With ceaseless and disconsolate conceits,
    Which dies my looks so lifeless as they are,   15
    And might, if my extremes had full events,
    Make me the ghastly counterfeit of death.

AGYDAS

    Eternal heaven sooner be dissolved,
    And all that pierceth Phoebe's silver eye,
    Before such hap fall to Zenocrate.   20

ZENOCRATE

    Ah, life and soul, still hover in his breast,
    And leave my body senseless as the earth.
    Or else unite you to his life and soul,
    That I may live and die with Tamburlaine.

      Enter [behind], TAMBURLAINE *with* TECHELLES *and others*

AGYDAS

    With Tamburlaine? Ah fair Zenocrate   25
    Let not a man so vile and barbarous,
    That holds you from your father in despite,
    And keeps you from the honours of a queen,
    Being supposed his worthless concubine,
    Be honoured with your love, but for necessity.   30
    So now the mighty Soldan hears of you,
    Your highness needs not doubt but in short time,
    He will with Tamburlaine's destruction
    Redeem you from this deadly servitude.

ZENOCRATE

    [Agydas,] leave to wound me with these words,   35
    And speak of Tamburlaine as he deserves:

11 *Queen of Heaven* Juno
14 *conceits* fancies
16 *extremes* violent passions
16 *events* expression in action
17 *counterfeit* likeness
19 *all . . . eye* all that the moon beholds
24 s.d. *[behind],* ed. (O1 omits)
31 *So* provided that
35 *[Agydas,] leave* ed. (Leave O1)

The entertainment we have had of him,
Is far from villainy or servitude,
And might in noble minds be counted princely.

AGYDAS
How can you fancy one that looks so fierce,   40
Only disposed to martial stratagems?
Who when he shall embrace you in his arms,
Will tell how many thousand men he slew,
And when you look for amorous discourse,
Will rattle forth his facts of war and blood,   45
Too harsh a subject for your dainty ears.

ZENOCRATE
As looks the sun through Nilus' flowing stream,
Or when the morning holds him in her arms,
So looks my lordly love, fair Tamburlaine:
His talk much sweeter than the Muses' song,   50
They sung for honour 'gainst Pierides,
Or when Minerva did with Neptune strive,
And higher would I rear my estimate,
Than Juno, sister to the highest god,
If I were matched with mighty Tamburlaine.   55

AGYDAS
Yet be not so inconstant in your love,
But let the young Arabian live in hope,
After your rescue to enjoy his choice.
You see though first the King of Persia
(Being a shepherd) seemed to love you much,   60
Now in his majesty he leaves those looks,
Those words of favour, and those comfortings,
And gives no more than common courtesies.

ZENOCRATE
Thence rise the tears that so distain my cheeks,
Fearing his love through my unworthiness.   65

> TAMBURLAINE *goes to her, and takes her away lovingly by the*
> *hand, looking wrathfully on* AGYDAS, *and says nothing.*
>   [*Exeunt all except* AGYDAS]

37 *entertainment* treatment
38 *villainy* dishonour   40 *fancy* love
52 *Minerva . . . strive* strive for control of Athens
65 *Fearing his love* fearing to lose his love
s.d. [*Exeunt . . .* AGYDAS] ed. (O1 omits)

50–1 The nine daughters of King Pierus were defeated by the Muses in a
singing contest and transformed into birds.

AGYDAS

Betrayed by fortune and suspicious love,
Threatened with frowning wrath and jealousy,
Surprised with fear of hideous revenge,
I stand aghast: but most astonied
To see his choler shut in secret thoughts,   70
And wrapped in silence of his angry soul.
Upon his brows was portrayed ugly death,
And in his eyes the fury of his heart,
That shine as comets, menacing revenge,
And casts a pale complexion on his cheeks.   75
As when the seaman sees the Hyades
Gather an army of Cimmerian clouds
(Auster and Aquilon with winged steeds
All sweating, tilt about the watery heavens,
With shivering spears enforcing thunderclaps,   80
And from their shields strike flames of lightening),
All-fearful folds his sails and sounds the main,
Lifting his prayers to the heavens for aid,
Against the terror of the winds and waves:
So fares Agydas for the late-felt frowns   85
That sent a tempest to my daunted thoughts,
And makes my soul divine her overthrow.

Enter TECHELLES *with a naked dagger* [*and* USUMCASANE]

TECHELLES

See you Agydas how the king salutes you.
He bids you prophesy what it imports.

AGYDAS

I prophesied before and now I prove,   90
The killing frowns of jealousy and love.

69 *astonied* astonished
74 *comets* the signs of disaster
78 *Auster* the south wind
78 *Aquilon* the north wind
79 *tilt* fight
82 *sounds the main* measures the depth of the sea
87 s.d. [*and* USUMCASANE] ed. (O1 omits)
89 *imports* O3–4 (imports. *Exit* O1)
90 *prove* find by experience

76 *Hyades*. A constellation of seven stars which were supposed to bring
rain if they rose at the same time as the sun.
77 *Cimmerian*. Dark. The Cimmerii were said to live in perpetual darkness.

He needed not with words confirm my fear,
For words are vain where working tools present
The naked action of my threatened end.
It says, Agydas, thou shalt surely die,   95
And of extremities elect the least.
More honour and less pain it may procure,
To die by this resolved hand of thine,
Than stay the torments he and heaven have sworn.
Then haste Agydas, and prevent the plagues: 100
Which thy prolonged fates may draw on thee:
Go wander free from fear of tyrant's rage,
Removed from the torments and the hell:
Wherewith he may excruciate thy soul.
And let Agydas by Agydas die,   105
And with this stab slumber eternally.
                                        [*Stabs himself*]

TECHELLES
    Usumcasane, see how right the man
    Hath hit the meaning of my lord the king.
USUMCASANE
    Faith, and Techelles, it was manly done:
    And since he was so wise and honourable,   110
    Let us afford him now the bearing hence,
    And crave his triple-worthy burial.
TECHELLES
    Agreed Casane, we will honour him.
                        [*Exeunt, bearing out the body*]

Act III, Scene iii

[*Enter*] TAMBURLAINE, TECHELLES, USUMCASANE, THERIDAMAS,
                BASSO, ZENOCRATE, *with others*

TAMBURLAINE
    Basso, by this thy lord and master knows,
    I mean to meet him in Bithynia:
    See how he comes! Tush, Turks are full of brags
    And manage more than they can well perform:
    He meet me in the field and fetch thee hence?   5

99 *stay* await
106 s.d. O4 (O1 omits)
113 s.d. ed. (O1 omits)

2 *Bithynia*. A district in Asia Minor south of the Black Sea.

Alas, poor Turk, his fortune is too weak,
T'encounter with the strength of Tamburlaine.
View well my camp, and speak indifferently,
Do not my captains and my soldiers look
As if they meant to conquer Africa?   10

BASSO

Your men are valiant but their number few,
And cannot terrify his mighty host.
My lord, the great commander of the world,
Besides fifteen contributory kings,
Hath now in arms ten thousand janissaries,   15
Mounted on lusty Mauritanian steeds:
Brought to the war by men of Tripoly.
Two hundred thousand footmen that have served
In two set battles fought in Graecia:
And for the expedition of this war,   20
If he think good, can from his garrisons,
Withdraw as many more to follow him.

TECHELLES

The more he brings, the greater is the spoil,
For when they perish by our warlike hands,
We mean to seat our footmen on their steeds,   25
And rifle all those stately janissars.

TAMBURLAINE

But will those kings accompany your lord?

BASSO

Such as his highness please, but some must stay
To rule the provinces he late subdued.

TAMBURLAINE

Then fight courageously, their crowns are yours.   30
This hand shall set them on your conquering heads:
That made me emperor of Asia.

USUMCASANE

Let him bring millions infinite of men,
Unpeopling western Africa and Greece:
Yet we assure us of the victory.   35

THERIDAMAS

Even he that in a trice vanquished two kings,

 8 *indifferently* without prejudice
15 *janissaries* Turkish infantry
29 *late* lately

---

16 *Mauritanian steeds*. Mauritania in north-west Africa on the Barbary
coast was famous for its horses.

More mighty than the Turkish emperor:
Shall rouse him out of Europe, and pursue
His scattered army till they yield or die.

TAMBURLAINE

Well said Theridamas, speak in that mood,　　　　　　　40
For 'will' and 'shall' best fitteth Tamburlaine,
Whose smiling stars gives him assured hope
Of martial triumph, ere he meet his foes:
I that am termed the Scourge and Wrath of God,
The only fear and terror of the world,　　　　　　　　45
Will first subdue the Turk, and then enlarge
Those Christian captives, which you keep as slaves,
Burdening their bodies with your heavy chains,
And feeding them with thin and slender fare,
That naked row about the Terrene sea.　　　　　　　50
And when they chance to breathe and rest a space,
Are punished with bastones so grievously,
That they lie panting on the galley's side,
And strive for life at every stroke they give.
These are the cruel pirates of Argier,　　　　　　　55
That damned train, the scum of Africa,
Inhabited with straggling runagates,
That make quick havoc of the Christian blood.
But as I live that town shall curse the time
That Tamburlaine set foot in Africa.　　　　　　　60

Enter BAJAZETH *with his Bassoes and contributory Kings* [*of* FEZ,
　　　MOROCCO, *and* ARGIER, ZABINA *and* EBEA]

BAJAZETH

Bassoes and janissaries of my guard,
Attend upon the person of your lord,
The greatest potentate of Africa.

TAMBURLAINE

Techelles, and the rest prepare your swords.
I mean t'encounter with that Bajazeth.　　　　　　　65

BAJAZETH

Kings of Fez, Morocco and Argier,
He calls me Bajazeth, whom you call lord!
Note the presumption of this Scythian slave:

46 *enlarge* set free
52 *bastones* cudgels
56 *train* troop
57 *runagates* apostates, deserters
66 *Morocco* ed. (Moroccus O1)

I tell thee villain, those that lead my horse
Have to their names titles of dignity,   70
And dar'st thou bluntly call me Bajazeth?

TAMBURLAINE
And know thou Turk, that those which lead my horse,
Shall lead thee captive thorough Africa.
And dar'st thou bluntly call me Tamburlaine?

BAJAZETH
By Mahomet my kinsman's sepulcher,   75
And by the holy Alçoran I swear,
He shall be made a chaste and lustless eunuch,
And in my sarell tend my concubines:
And all his captains that thus stoutly stand,
Shall draw the chariot of my emperess,   80
Whom I have brought to see their overthrow.

TAMBURLAINE
By this my sword that conquered Persia,
Thy fall shall make me famous through the world:
I will not tell thee how I'll handle thee,
But every common soldier of my camp   85
Shall smile to see thy miserable state.

KING OF FEZ
What means the mighty Turkish emperor
To talk with one so base as Tamburlaine?

KING OF MOROCCO
Ye Moors and valiant men of Barbary,
How can ye suffer these indignities?   90

KING OF ARGIER
Leave words and let them feel your lances' points,
Which glided through the bowels of the Greeks.

BAJAZETH
Well said my stout contributory kings,
Your threefold army and my hugy host,
Shall swallow up these base-born Persians.   95

TECHELLES
Puissant, renowned and mighty Tamburlaine,
Why stay we thus prolonging all their lives?

THERIDAMAS
I long to see those crowns won by our swords
That we may reign as kings of Africa.

70 *to* in addition to
78 *sarell* seraglio, harem
94 *hugy* huge

USUMCASANE
  What coward would not fight for such a prize?   100
TAMBURLAINE
  Fight all courageously and be you kings.
  I speak it, and my words are oracles.
BAJAZETH
  Zabina, mother of three braver boys,
  Than Hercules, that in his infancy
  Did pash the jaws of serpents venomous: 105
  Whose hands are made to gripe a warlike lance,
  Their shoulders broad, for complete armour fit,
  Their limbs more large and of a bigger size
  Than all the brats ysprung from Typhon's loins:
  Who, when they come unto their father's age,   110
  Will batter turrets with their manly fists:
  Sit here upon this royal chair of state,
  And on thy head wear my imperial crown,
  Until I bring this sturdy Tamburlaine,
  And all his captains bound in captive chains.   115
ZABINA
  Such good success happen to Bajazeth.
TAMBURLAINE
  Zenocrate, the loveliest maid alive,
  Fairer than rocks of pearl and precious stone,
  The only paragon of Tamburlaine,
  Whose eyes are brighter than the lamps of heaven   120
  And speech more pleasant than sweet harmony:
  That with thy looks canst clear the darkened sky:
  And calm the rage of thundering Jupiter:
  Sit down by her: adorned with my crown,
  As if thou wert the empress of the world.   125
  Stir not Zenocrate until thou see
  Me march victoriously with all my men,
  Triumphing over him and these his kings,
  Which I will bring as vassals to thy feet.
  Till then take thou my crown, vaunt of my worth,   130
  And manage words with her as we will arms.

105 *pash* smash, crush   109 *ysprung* sprung
119 *paragon* match, consort
131 *manage ... arms* fight her with words as we shall fight with
    weapons

---

109 *Typhon's.* Typhon or Typhaon was a hundred-headed giant, the father
   of various monsters.

ZENOCRATE
And may my love, the King of Persia,
Return with victory, and free from wound.

BAJAZETH
Now shalt thou feel the force of Turkish arms,
Which lately made all Europe quake for fear: 135
I have of Turks, Arabians, Moors and Jews
Enough to cover all Bithynia.
Let thousands die, their slaughtered carcasses
Shall serve for walls and bulwarks to the rest:
And as the heads of Hydra, so my power   140
Subdued, shall stand as mighty as before:
If they should yield their necks unto the sword,
Thy soldiers' arms could not endure to strike
So many blows as I have heads for thee.
Thou knowest not, foolish-hardy Tamburlaine,   145
What 'tis to meet me in the open field,
That leave no ground for thee to march upon.

TAMBURLAINE
Our conquering swords shall marshal us the way
We use to march upon the slaughtered foe:
Trampling their bowels with our horses' hoofs: 150
Brave horses, bred on the white Tartarian hills:
My camp is like to Julius Caesar's host,
That never fought but had the victory:
Nor in Pharsalia was there such hot war,
As these my followers willingly would have: 155
Legions of spirits fleeting in the air,
Direct our bullets and our weapons' points
And make our strokes to wound the senseless lure,
And when she sees our bloody colours spread,
Then Victory begins to take her flight,   160
Resting herself upon my milk-white tent.

---

140 *Hydra* a hundred-headed monster
148 *marshal* point out, lead

---

154 *Pharsalia*. Julius Caesar defeated Pompey in 48 B.C. at the battle of
  Pharsalus.
158 *lure*. 'An apparatus used by falconers to recall their hawks, constructed
  of a bunch of feathers, to which is attached a long cord or thong, and
  from the interstices of which, during its training, the hawk is fed'
  (*O.E.D.*). Tamburlaine regards his adversaries as imitation men, just
  as the lure is the imitation of a bird.

But come my lords, to weapons let us fall.
The field is ours, the Turk, his wife and all.

Exit, with his followers

BAJAZETH
Come kings and bassoes, let us glut our swords
That thirst to drink the feeble Persians' blood.   165

Exit, with his followers

ZABINA
Base concubine, must thou be placed by me
That am the empress of the mighty Turk?

ZENOCRATE
Disdainful Turkess and unreverend boss,
Call'st thou me concubine that am betrothed
Unto the great and mighty Tamburlaine?   170

ZABINA
To Tamburlaine the great Tartarian thief?

ZENOCRATE
Thou wilt repent these lavish words of thine,
When thy great basso-master and thyself
Must plead for mercy at his kingly feet,
And sue to me to be your advocates.   175

ZABINA
And sue to thee? I tell thee shameless girl,
Thou shalt be laundress to my waiting-maid.
How lik'st thou her Ebea, will she serve?

EBEA
Madam, she thinks perhaps she is too fine.
But I shall turn her into other weeds,   180
And make her dainty fingers fall to work.

ZENOCRATE
Hear'st thou Anippe, how thy drudge doth talk,
And how my slave, her mistress, menaceth.
Both for their sauciness shall be employed,
To dress the common soldiers' meat and drink.   185
For we will scorn they should come near ourselves.

ANIPPE
Yet sometimes let your highness send for them
To do the work my chambermaid disdains.

They sound to the battle within, and stay

ZENOCRATE
Ye gods and powers that govern Persia:

168 *unreverend boss* irreverent fat woman
175 *advocates* possibly 'advocatess' (a feminine form)
180 *weeds* clothing

And made my lordly love her worthy king: 190
Now strengthen him against the Turkish Bajazeth,
And let his foes like flocks of fearful roes,
Pursued by hunters, fly his angry looks,
That I may see him issue conqueror.

ZABINA
Now Mahomet, solicit God himself,   195
And make him rain down murdering shot from heaven
To dash the Scythians' brains, and strike them dead,
That dare to manage arms with him,
That offered jewels to thy sacred shrine,
When first he warred against the Christians.   200

To the battle again

ZENOCRATE
By this the Turks lie weltering in their blood
And Tamburlaine is lord of Africa.

ZABINA
Thou art deceived, I heard the trumpets sound
As when my emperor overthrew the Greeks:
And led them captive into Africa.   205
Straight will I use thee as thy pride deserves:
Prepare thyself to live and die my slave.

ZENOCRATE
If Mahomet should come from heaven and swear,
My royal lord is slain or conquered,
Yet should he not persuade me otherwise,   210
But that he lives and will be conqueror.

BAJAZETH *flies and* [TAMBURLAINE] *pursues him. The battle
short, and they enter.* BAJAZETH *is overcome*

TAMBURLAINE
Now king of bassoes, who is conqueror?
BAJAZETH
Thou, by the fortune of this damned foil.
TAMBURLAINE
Where are your stout contributory kings?

Enter TECHELLES, THERIDAMAS, USUMCASANE

TECHELLES
We have their crowns, their bodies strew the field.   215

196 *murdering* ed. (murthering O1)
211 s.d. [TAMBURLAINE] ed. (he O1)
213 *foil* ed. (soile O1) defeat

TAMBURLAINE
Each man a crown? Why kingly fought i'faith.
Deliver them into my treasury.

ZENOCRATE
Now let me offer to my gracious lord
His royal crown again, so highly won.

TAMBURLAINE
Nay take the Turkish crown from her, Zenocrate,   220
And crown me emperor of Africa.

ZABINA
No Tamburlaine, though now thou gat the best
Thou shalt not yet be lord of Africa.

THERIDAMAS
Give her the crown, Turkess, you were best.
                He takes it from her and gives it to ZENOCRATE

ZABINA
Injurious villains, thieves, runagates,   225
How dare you thus abuse my majesty?

THERIDAMAS
Here madam, you are empress, she is none.

TAMBURLAINE
Not now Theridamas, her time is past:
The pillars that have bolstered up those terms,
Are fallen in clusters at my conquering feet.   230

ZABINA
Though he be prisoner, he may be ransomed.

TAMBURLAINE
Not all the world shall ransom Bajazeth.

BAJAZETH
Ah fair Zabina, we have lost the field.
And never had the Turkish emperor
So great a foil by any foreign foe.   235
Now will the Christian miscreants be glad,
Ringing with joy their superstitious bells:
And making bonfires for my overthrow.
But ere I die those foul idolators
Shall make me bonfires with their filthy bones,   240
For though the glory of this day be lost,
Afric and Greece have garrisons enough
To make me sovereign of the earth again.

220 *Zenocrate* ed. (Zen. O1)
222 *gat the best* got the upper hand
225 *runagates* vagabonds
229 *terms* statuary busts set on pillars

TAMBURLAINE

Those walled garrisons will I subdue,
And write myself great lord of Africa: 245
So from the East unto the furtherest West,
Shall Tamburlaine extend his puissant arm.
The galleys and those pilling brigandines,
That yearly sail to the Venetian gulf,
And hover in the straits for Christians' wrack,   250
Shall lie at anchor in the Isle Asant,
Until the Persian fleet and men-of-war,
Sailing along the oriental sea,
Have fetched about the Indian continent:
Even from Persepolis to Mexico,   255
And thence unto the Straits of Jubalter:
Where they shall meet, and join their force in one,
Keeping in awe the Bay of Portingale,
And all the ocean by the British shore:
And by this means I'll win the world at last.   260

BAJAZETH

Yet set a ransom on me Tamburlaine.

TAMBURLAINE

What, think'st thou Tamburlaine esteems thy gold?
I'll make the kings of India ere I die,
Offer their mines (to sue for peace) to me,
And dig for treasure to appease my wrath: 265
Come bind them both and one lead in the Turk.
The Turkess let my love's maid lead away.

They bind them

BAJAZETH

Ah villains, dare ye touch my sacred arms?
O Mahomet, O sleepy Mahomet!

ZABINA

O cursed Mahomet that makest us thus   270
The slaves to Scythians rude and barbarous!

TAMBURLAINE

Come bring them in, and for this happy conquest
Triumph, and solemnize a martial feast.

Exeunt

---

248 *pilling brigandines* pillaging brigantines
250 *wrack* destruction   254 *fetched about* circumnavigated
256 *Jubalter* Gibraltar

---

251 *Isle Asant*. Zante, off the coast of Achaia.
258 *Bay of Portingale*. Bay of Biscay.

Act IV, Scene i

[*Enter*] SOLDAN OF EGYPT, *with three or four Lords*, CAPOLIN,
[MESSENGER]

SOLDAN

Awake ye men of Memphis, hear the clang
Of Scythian trumpets, hear the basilisks,
That roaring, shake Damascus' turrets down!
The rogue of Volga holds Zenocrate,
The Soldan's daughter for his concubine,   5
And with a troop of thieves and vagabonds,
Hath spread his colours to our high disgrace:
While you faint-hearted base Egyptians,
Lie slumbering on the flowery banks of Nile,
As crocodiles that unaffrighted rest,   10
While thundering cannons rattle on their skins.

MESSENGER

Nay, mighty Soldan, did your greatness see
The frowning looks of mighty Tamburlaine,
That with his terror and imperious eyes,
Commands the hearts of his associates,   15
It might amaze your royal majesty.

SOLDAN

Villain, I tell thee, were that Tamburlaine
As monstrous as Gorgon, prince of hell,
The Soldan would not start a foot from him.
But speak, what power hath he?
MESSENGER   Mighty lord,   20
Three hundred thousand men in armour clad,
Upon their prancing steeds, disdainfully
With wanton paces trampling on the ground.
Five hundred thousand footmen threatening shot,
Shaking their swords, their spears and iron bills,   25
Environing their standard round, that stood
As bristle-pointed as a thorny wood.
Their warlike engines and munition
Exceed the forces of their martial men.

2 *basilisks* large cannons
12 s.p. ed. (O1 omits)
23 *wanton* sportive
25 *bills* axes

---

18 *Gorgon.* Demogorgon, a devil.

SOLDAN

 Nay could their numbers countervail the stars   30
 Or ever-drizzling drops of April showers,
 Or withered leaves that autumn shaketh down:
 Yet would the Soldan by his conquering power,
 So scatter and consume them in his rage,
 That not a man shall live to rue their fall.   35

CAPOLIN

 So might your highness, had you time to sort
 Your fighting men, and raise your royal host.
 But Tamburlaine, by expedition
 Advantage takes of your unreadiness.

SOLDAN

 Let him take all th'advantages he can;   40
 Were all the world conspired to fight for him,
 Nay, were he devil, as he is no man,
 Yet in revenge of fair Zenocrate,
 Whom he detaineth in despite of us,
 This arm should send him down to Erebus,   45
 To shroud his shame in darkness of the night.

MESSENGER

 Pleaseth your mightiness to understand,
 His resolution far exceedeth all:
 The first day when he pitcheth down his tents,
 White is their hue, and on his silver crest   50
 A snowy feather spangled white he bears,
 To signify the mildness of his mind,
 That satiate with spoil refuseth blood:
 But when Aurora mounts the second time,
 As red as scarlet is his furniture,   55
 Then must his kindled wrath be quenched with blood,
 Not sparing any that can manage arms:
 But if these threats move not submission,
 Black are his colours, black pavilion,
 His spear, his shield, his horse, his armour, plumes, 60
 And jetty feathers menace death and hell.
 Without respect of sex, degree or age,
 He razeth all his foes with fire and sword.

30 *countervail* equal in number 38 *expedition* speed
54 *Aurora* goddess of the dawn
55 *furniture* military equipment

---

45 *Erebus.* The son of Chaos and the brother of Night, ruler of the dark
region beneath the earth.

SOLDAN
    Merciless villain, peasant ignorant
    Of lawful arms, or martial discipline: 65
    Pillage and murder are his usual trades!
    The slave usurps the glorious name of war.
    See, Capolin, the fair Arabian king
    That hath been disappointed by this slave
    Of my fair daughter and his princely love,   70
    May have fresh warning to go to war with us,
    And be revenged for her disparagement.   [*Exeunt*]

Act IV, Scene ii

[*Enter*] TAMBURLAINE, TECHELLES, THERIDAMAS, USUMCASANE,
ZENOCRATE, ANIPPE, *two Moors drawing* BAJAZETH *in his cage, and
his wife* [ZABINA] *following him*

TAMBURLAINE
    Bring out my footstool.
                                They take him out of the cage
BAJAZETH
    Ye holy priests of heavenly Mahomet,
    That sacrificing slice and cut your flesh,
    Staining his altars with your purple blood:
    Make heaven to frown and every fixed star   5
    To suck up poison from the moorish fens,
    And pour it in this glorious tyrant's throat!
TAMBURLAINE
    The chiefest god, first mover of that sphere
    Enchased with thousands ever-shining lamps,
    Will sooner burn the glorious frame of heaven,   10
    Than it should so conspire my overthrow.
    But villain, thou that wishest this to me,
    Fall prostrate on the low disdainful earth,
    And be the footstool of great Tamburlaine,
    That I may rise into my royal throne.   15
BAJAZETH
    First shalt thou rip my bowels with thy sword,

72 s.d. ed. (O1 omits)
7 *glorious* boastful

8–9 *chiefest god . . . lamps.* The Aristotelian conception of God as the
'prime mover', who initiates the movement of the 'primum mobile', or
outermost sphere whose motion causes that of the other heavenly
spheres.

And sacrifice my heart to death and hell,
Before I yield to such a slavery.

TAMBURLAINE
Base villain, vassal, slave to Tamburlaine:
Unworthy to embrace or touch the ground,   20
That bears the honour of my royal weight!
Stoop villain, stoop! Stoop, for so he bids,
That may command thee piecemeal to be torn,
Or scattered like the lofty cedar trees,
Struck with the voice of thundering Jupiter.   25

BAJAZETH
Then as I look down to the damned fiends,
Fiends look on me, and thou dread god of hell,
With ebon sceptre strike this hateful earth,
And make it swallow both of us at once!

            TAMBURLAINE *gets up upon him to his chair*

TAMBURLAINE
Now clear the triple region of the air,   30
And let the majesty of heaven behold
Their scourge and terror tread on emperors.
Smile stars that reigned at my nativity:
And dim the brightness of their neighbour lamps,
Disdain to borrow light of Cynthia,   35
For I the chiefest lamp of all the earth,
First rising in the east with mild aspect,
But fixed now in the meridian line,
Will send up fire to your turning spheres,
And cause the sun to borrow light of you.   40
My sword struck fire from his coat of steel,
Even in Bithynia, when I took this Turk:
As when a fiery exhalation
Wrapped in the bowels of a freezing cloud,

17 *heart* O1, O3–4 (soule O2)
35 *Cynthia* the moon
43 *exhalation* a vapour drawn from the earth's atmosphere

30 *triple . . . air.* An allusion to the contemporary belief that the air,
between the earth and the sphere of fire, was divided into three 'regions'
according to distance from the earth and temperature.
38 *the meridian line.* An imaginary arc through the sky, running from north
to south directly above the observer's head so that the sun passed
through it at noon. Tamburlaine has reached the high noon of his
fortunes; but if his word 'fixed' implies that he expects to remain there
eternally, such an assertion would contravene contemporary views
concerning the natural order.

Fighting for passage, makes the welkin crack,   45
And casts a flash of lightning to the earth.
But ere I march to wealthy Persia,
Or leave Damascus and the Egyptian fields,
As was the fame of Clymene's brain-sick son,
That almost brent the axle-tree of heaven,   50
So shall our swords, our lances and our shot
Fill all the air with fiery meteors.
Then when the sky shall wax as red as blood,
It shall be said, I made it red myself,
To make me think of naught but blood and war.   55
ZABINA
Unworthy king, that by thy cruelty,
Unlawfully usurpest the Persian seat:
Dar'st thou that never saw an emperor,
Before thou met my husband in the field,
Being thy captive, thus abuse his state,   60
Keeping his kingly body in a cage,
That roofs of gold, and sun-bright palaces,
Should have prepared to entertain his grace?
And treading him beneath thy loathsome feet,
Whose feet the kings of Africa have kissed?   65
TECHELLES
You must devise some torment worse, my lord,
To make these captives rein their lavish tongues.
TAMBURLAINE
Zenocrate, look better to your slave.
ZENOCRATE
She is my handmaid's slave, and she shall look
That these abuses flow not from her tongue: 70
Chide her Anippe.
ANIPPE
Let these be warnings for you then my slave,

45 *makes* ed. (make O1)
45 *welkin* sky
49 *Clymene's* O2 (Clymeus O1)
50 *brent* burnt
50 *axle-tree of heaven* the axis of the universe on which all of the
   heavenly spheres were believed to turn
60 *state* high rank
67 *lavish* free-speaking

---

49 *Clymene's . . . son.* Phaëton, son of Clymene and the sun god, Apollo,
   met disaster when he tried to drive his father's horses across the sky.

How you abuse the person of the king:
Or else I swear to have you whipped stark naked.

BAJAZETH

Great Tamburlaine, great in my overthrow,   75
Ambitious pride shall make thee fall as low,
For treading on the back of Bajazeth,
That should be horsed on four mighty kings.

TAMBURLAINE

Thy names and titles, and thy dignities
Are fled from Bajazeth, and remain with me,   80
That will maintain it against a world of kings.
Put him in again.

> [*They put him into the cage*]

BAJAZETH

Is this a place for mighty Bajazeth?
Confusion light on him that helps thee thus.

TAMBURLAINE

There whiles he lives, shall Bajazeth be kept   85
And where I go be thus in triumph drawn
And thou his wife shall feed him with the scraps
My servitors shall bring thee from my board.
For he that gives him other food than this:
Shall sit by him and starve to death himself.   90
This is my mind, and I will have it so.
Not all the kings and emperors of the earth:
If they would lay their crowns before my feet,
Shall ransom him, or take him from his cage.
The ages that shall talk of Tamburlaine,   95
Even from this day to Plato's wondrous year,
Shall talk how I have handled Bajazeth.
These Moors that drew him from Bithynia,
To fair Damascus, where we now remain,
Shall lead him with us wheresoe'er we go.   100
Techelles, and my loving followers,
Now may we see Damascus' lofty towers,
Like to the shadows of Pyramides,

82 s.d. ed. (O1 omits)
88 *servitors* ed. (seruitures O1)

---

96 *Plato's wondrous year*. In *Timaeus* (39 D) Plato writes of the future year
    when all of the planets will have returned to their original positions.
102–3 *towers . . . Pyramides*. Towers which are mere shadows of the great
    Pyramids. The word 'pyramides' could refer to any structure of
    pyramidal form, such as obelisks.

That with their beauties graced the Memphian fields:
The golden statue of their feathered bird   105
That spreads her wings upon the city walls,
Shall not defend it from our battering shot.
The townsmen mask in silk and cloth of gold,
And every house is as a treasury.
The men, the treasure, and the town is ours.   110

THERIDAMAS

Your tents of white now pitched before the gates
And gentle flags of amity displayed,
I doubt not but the governor will yield,
Offering Damascus to your majesty.

TAMBURLAINE

So shall he have his life, and all the rest.   115
But if he stay until the bloody flag
Be once advanced on my vermillion tent,
He dies, and those that kept us out so long.
And when they see me march in black array,
With mournful streamers hanging down their heads,   120
Were in that city all the world contained,
Not one should 'scape: but perish by our swords.

ZENOCRATE

Yet would you have some pity for my sake,
Because it is my country's and my father's.

TAMBURLAINE

Not for the world Zenocrate, if I have sworn: 125
Come bring in the Turk.   *Exeunt*

Act IV, Scene iii

[*Enter*] SOLDAN, [KING OF] ARABIA, CAPOLIN, *with streaming
colours; and Soldiers*

SOLDAN

Methinks we march as Meleager did,
Environed with brave Argolian knights,
To chase the savage Calydonian boar,

105 *statue* O3–4 (stature O1)   105 *bird* the eagle
108 *mask* dress   116 *stay* wait
120 *streamers* pennons   124 *it* i.e., the city
   s.d. *streaming* O3–4 (steaming O1)
   3 *Calydonian* O2 (Caldonian O1)

1–2 *Meleager . . . Argolian knights.* Meleager was a Greek hero who killed
   the monstrous Calydonian boar after returning home from the Argo-
   nautic expedition.

Or Cephalus with lusty Theban youths
Against the wolf that angry Themis sent,   5
To waste and spoil the sweet Aonian fields.
A monster of five hundred thousand heads,
Compact of rapine, piracy and spoil,
The scum of men, the hate and scourge of God,
Raves in Egyptia, and annoyeth us.   10
My lord it is the bloody Tamburlaine,
A sturdy felon and a base-born thief,
By murder raised to the Persian crown,
That dares control us in our territories.
To tame the pride of this presumptuous beast,   15
Join your Arabians with the Soldan's power:
Let us unite our royal bands in one,
And hasten to remove Damascus' siege.
It is a blemish to the majesty
And high estate of mighty emperors,   20
That such a base usurping vagabond
Should brave a king, or wear a princely crown.

KING OF ARABIA
Renowned Soldan, have ye lately heard
The overthrow of mighty Bajazeth,
About the confines of Bithynia?   25
The slavery wherewith he persecutes
The noble Turk and his great emperess?

SOLDAN
I have, and sorrow for his bad success:
But noble lord of great Arabia,
Be so persuaded, that the Soldan is   30
No more dismayed with tidings of his fall,
Than in the haven where the pilot stands
And views a stranger ship rent in the winds,
And shivered against a craggy rock;
Yet in compassion of his wretched state,   35
A sacred vow to heaven and him I make,

---

6 *Aonian* Theban
14 *control* overpower
25 *confines* borders
28 *bad success* ill fortune

---

4 *Cephalus*. A hunter who destroyed a wild beast that was ravaging the
   Theban territories.
5 *Themis*. A Greek deity, the symbol of order and justice.

Confirming it with Ibis' holy name,
That Tamburlaine shall rue the day, the hour,
Wherein he wrought such ignominious wrong
Unto the hallowed person of a prince,   40
Or kept the fair Zenocrate so long,
As concubine, I fear, to feed his lust.

KING OF ARABIA

Let grief and fury hasten on revenge,
Let Tamburlaine for his offences feel
Such plagues as heaven and we can pour on him.   45
I long to break my spear upon his crest,
And prove the weight of his victorious arm:
For fame I fear hath been too prodigal
In sounding through the world his partial praise.

SOLDAN

Capolin, hast thou surveyed our powers?   50

CAPOLIN

Great emperors of Egypt and Arabia
The number of your hosts united is,
A hundred and fifty thousand horse,
Two hundred thousand foot, brave men-at-arms,
Courageous and full of hardiness: 55
As frolic as the hunters in the chase
Of savage beasts amid the desert woods.

KING OF ARABIA

My mind presageth fortunate success,
And Tamburlaine, my spirit doth foresee
The utter ruin of thy men and thee.   60

SOLDAN

Then rear your standards, let your sounding drums
Direct our soldiers to Damascus' walls.
Now Tamburlaine, the mighty Soldan comes,
And leads with him the great Arabian king,
To dim thy baseness and obscurity,   65
Famous for nothing but for theft and spoil;
To raze and scatter thy inglorious crew,
Of Scythians and slavish Persians.   *Exeunt*

37 *Ibis* a bird held sacred by the Egyptians
47 *prove* test
49 *partial* biased, prejudiced
56 *frolic* merry

---

65 *thy baseness and obscurity.* Reference to Tamburlaine's low birth, which
some of Marlowe's sources emphasized and exaggerated.

Act IV, Scene iv

The banquet, and to it cometh TAMBURLAINE *all in scarlet,* [ZENO-CRATE], THERIDAMAS, TECHELLES, USUMCASANE, *the Turk* [BAJAZETH, *in his cage,* ZABINA], *with others*

TAMBURLAINE
Now hang our bloody colours by Damascus,
Reflexing hues of blood upon their heads,
While they walk quivering on their city walls,
Half dead for fear before they feel my wrath:
Then let us freely banquet and carouse   5
Full bowls of wine unto the god of war,
That means to fill your helmets full of gold:
And make Damascus' spoils as rich to you,
As was to Jason Colchos' golden fleece.
And now Bajazeth, hast thou any stomach?   10

BAJAZETH
Ay, such a stomach, cruel Tamburlaine, as I could
Willingly feed upon thy blood-red heart.

TAMBURLAINE
Nay, thine own is easier to come by, pluck out that,
And 'twill serve thee and thy wife. Well Zenocrate,
Techelles and the rest, fall to your victuals.   15

BAJAZETH
Fall to, and never may your meat digest!
Ye Furies that can mask invisible,
Dive to the bottom of Avernus' pool,
And in your hands bring hellish poison up,
And squeeze it in the cup of Tamburlaine.   20
Or winged snakes of Lerna cast your stings,
And leave your venoms in this tyrant's dish.

ZABINA
And may this banquet prove as ominous

---

2 *Reflexing* casting
10 *stomach* (1) hunger, (2) anger (since choler was thought to be
produced in the stomach)

---

9 *Jason.* Greek hero who led his Argonauts to Colchis in quest of the
golden fleece.
17 *Furies.* See note to II, vii, 53 above.
18 *Avernus' pool.* See note to I, ii, 160 above.
21 *Lerna.* A region near Argos where Hercules killed the Hydra.

As Progne's to th'adulterous Thracian king,
That fed upon the substance of his child.   25
ZENOCRATE
My lord, how can you suffer these
Outrageous curses by these slaves of yours?
TAMBURLAINE
To let them see, divine Zenocrate,
I glory in the curses of my foes,
Having the power from the empyreal heaven,   30
To turn them all upon their proper heads.
TECHELLES
I pray you give them leave madam, this speech is a goodly
refreshing to them.
THERIDAMAS
But if his highness would let them be fed, it would do them
more good.   35
TAMBURLAINE
Sirrah, why fall you not to? Are you so daintily brought up,
you cannot eat your own flesh?
BAJAZETH
First legions of devils shall tear thee in pieces.
USUMCASANE
Villain, knowest thou to whom thou speakest?
TAMBURLAINE
O let him alone: here, eat sir, take it from my sword's point,   40
or I'll thrust it to thy heart.
                          He takes it and stamps upon it
THERIDAMAS
He stamps it under his feet my lord.
TAMBURLAINE
Take it up villain, and eat it, or I will make thee slice the
brawns of thy arms into carbonadoes, and eat them.
USUMCASANE
Nay, 'twere better he killed his wife, and then she shall be   45

26–7 lineation ed.
30 *empyreal heaven* see note to II, vii, 15 above
31 *proper* own
32 *leave* i.e., permission to speak
36 *daintily* over-nicely
44 *brawns* muscles   44 *carbonadoes* thin strips of meat

24–5 *Progne ... child.* After Tereus, King of Thrace, had raped his
sister-in-law, Philomela, his wife, Progne, revenged herself by tricking
him into eating the body of Itys, their son.

sure not to be starved, and he be provided for a month's
victual beforehand.

TAMBURLAINE

Here is my dagger, dispatch her while she is fat, for if she
live but a while longer, she will fall into a consumption with
fretting, and then she will not be worth the eating.   50

THERIDAMAS

Dost thou think that Mahomet will suffer this?

TECHELLES

'Tis like he will, when he cannot let it.

TAMBURLAINE

Go to, fall to your meat: what not a bit? Belike he hath not
been watered today, give him some drink.

They give him water to drink, and he flings it on the ground

Fast and welcome sir, while hunger make you eat. How now   55
Zenocrate, doth not the Turk and his wife make a goodly
show at a banquet?

ZENOCRATE

Yes, my lord.

THERIDAMAS

Methinks, 'tis a great deal better than a consort of music.

TAMBURLAINE

Yet music would do well to cheer up Zenocrate: pray thee   60
tell, why art thou so sad? If thou wilt have a song, the Turk
shall strain his voice: but why is it?

ZENOCRATE

My lord, to see my father's town besieged,
The country wasted where myself was born,
How can it but affect my very soul?   65
If any love remain in you my lord,
Or if my love unto your majesty
May merit favour at your highness' hands,
Then raise your siege from fair Damascus' walls,
And with my father take a friendly truce.   70

TAMBURLAINE

Zenocrate, were Egypt Jove's own land,
Yet would I with my sword make Jove to stoop.

51 *suffer* allow
52 *let* prevent
55 *while* until
59 *consort of music* company of musicians
62 *strain* raise, i.e., sing

I will confute those blind geographers
That make a triple region in the world,
Excluding regions which I mean to trace,   75
And with this pen reduce them to a map,
Calling the provinces, cities and towns
After my name and thine Zenocrate:
Here at Damascus will I make the point
That shall begin the perpendicular,   80
And wouldst thou have me buy thy father's love
With such a loss? Tell me Zenocrate.

ZENOCRATE
Honour still wait on happy Tamburlaine:
Yet give me leave to plead for him my lord.

TAMBURLAINE
Content thyself, his person shall be safe,   85
And all the friends of fair Zenocrate,
If with their lives they will be pleased to yield,
Or may be forced to make me emperor.
For Egypt and Arabia must be mine.
—Feed, you slave, thou may'st think thyself happy to be fed   90
from my trencher.

BAJAZETH
My empty stomach, full of idle heat,
Draws bloody humours from my feeble parts,
Preserving life, by hasting cruel death.
My veins are pale, my sinews hard and dry,   95
My joints benumbed, unless I eat, I die.

ZABINA
Eat, Bajazeth. Let us live in spite of them,
Looking some happy power will pity and enlarge us.

TAMBURLAINE
Here Turk, wilt thou have a clean trencher?

74 *triple region* i.e., Asia, Africa, and Europe
76 *this pen* i.e., his sword
83 *still* forever
91 *trencher* wooden platter
93 *humours* vital internal fluids
98 *Looking* hoping that
98 *happy* favourable
98 *enlarge* free

79–80 *Here...perpendicular.* Tamburlaine will so reconstruct the kingdoms
of the earth as to make the prime meridian pass through Damascus as
the world's most important city.

BAJAZETH
Ay tyrant, and more meat.   100
TAMBURLAINE
Soft sir, you must be dieted, too much eating will make you
surfeit.
THERIDAMAS
So it would my lord, especially having so small a walk, and so
little exercise.

Enter a second course of crowns

TAMBURLAINE
Theridamas, Techelles and Casane, here are the cates you   105
desire to finger, are they not?
THERIDAMAS
Ay, my lord, but none save kings must feed with these.
TECHELLES
'Tis enough for us to see them, and for Tamburlaine only to
enjoy them.
TAMBURLAINE
Well, here is now to the Soldan of Egypt, the King of Arabia,   110
and the Governor of Damascus. Now take these three
crowns, and pledge me, my contributory kings. I crown you
here, Theridamas, King of Argier: Techelles, King of Fez:
and Usumcasane, King of Morocco. How say you to this,
Turk? These are not your contributory kings.   115
BAJAZETH
Nor shall they long be thine, I warrant them.
TAMBURLAINE
Kings of Argier, Morocco, and of Fez:
You that have marched with happy Tamburlaine,
As far as from the frozen place of heaven,
Unto the watery morning's ruddy bower,   120
And thence by land unto the torrid zone,
Deserve these titles I endow you with
By valour and by magnanimity.
Your births shall be no blemish to your fame,
For virtue is the fount whence honour springs,   125
And they are worthy she investeth kings.

105 *cates* delicacies
114 *Morocco* ed. (Moroccus O1)
117 *Morocco* ed. (Moroccus O1)
120 *bower* O3–4 (hour O1)
123 *valour* ed. (value O1)
124 *births* humble origins   125 *virtue* power and ability

THERIDAMAS
  And since your highness hath so well vouchsafed,
  If we deserve them not with higher meeds
  Than erst our states and actions have retained,
  Then take them away again and make us slaves.   130
TAMBURLAINE
  Well said Theridamas. When holy fates
  Shall 'stablish me in strong Egyptia,
  We mean to travel to th'antarctic pole,
  Conquering the people underneath our feet,
  And be renowned, as never emperors were.   135
  Zenocrate, I will not crown thee yet,
  Until with greater honours I be graced.   [*Exeunt*]

Act V, Scene i

[*Enter*] the GOVERNOR OF DAMASCUS, *with three or four Citizens,*
    and four VIRGINS *with branches of laurel in their hands*

GOVERNOR OF DAMASCUS
  Still doth this man or rather god of war,
  Batter our walls, and beat our turrets down.
  And to resist with longer stubbornness,
  Or hope of rescue from the Soldan's power,
  Were but to bring our wilful overthrow,   5
  And make us desperate of our threatened lives:
  We see his tents have now been altered
  With terrors to the last and cruellest hue:
  His coal-black colours everywhere advanced,
  Threaten our city with a general spoil: 10
  And if we should with common rites of arms,
  Offer our safeties to his clemency,
  I fear the custom proper to his sword,
  Which he observes as parcel of his fame,
  Intending so to terrify the world,   15
  By any innovation or remorse

128 *meeds* merits
129 *erst* formerly
129 *retained* contained
133 *th'antarctic* ed. (th'Antatique O1)
134 *underneath our feet* leaving the southern hemisphere s.d. ed.
  (O1 omits)
 13 *proper . . . sword* which is a part of the code of war
 14 *parcel* an essential part

Will never be dispensed with till our deaths.
Therefore, for these our harmless virgins' sakes,
Whose honours and whose lives rely on him:
Let us have hope that their unspotted prayers,   20
Their blubbered cheeks and hearty humble moans
Will melt his fury into some remorse:
And use us like a loving conqueror.

FIRST VIRGIN
If humble suits or imprecations
(Uttered with tears of wretchedness and blood,   25
Shed from the heads and hearts of all our sex,
Some made your wives, and some your children),
Might have entreated your obdurate breasts,
To entertain some care of our securities,
Whiles only danger beat upon our walls,   30
These more than dangerous warrants of our death
Had never been erected as they be,
Nor you depend on such weak helps as we.

GOVERNOR OF DAMASCUS
Well, lovely virgins, think our country's care,
Our love of honour loath to be enthralled   35
To foreign powers, and rough imperious yokes:
Would not with too much cowardice or fear,
Before all hope of rescue were denied,
Submit yourselves and us to servitude.
Therefore in that your safeties and our own,   40
Your honours, liberties and lives were weighed
In equal care and balance with our own,
Endure as we the malice of our stars,
The wrath of Tamburlaine, and power of wars,
Or be the means the overweighing heavens   45
Have kept to qualify these hot extremes.
And bring us pardon in your cheerful looks.

SECOND VIRGIN
Then here before the majesty of heaven,
And holy patrons of Egyptia,
With knees and hearts submissive we entreat   50
Grace to our words and pity to our looks

21 *blubbered* tear-stained
21 *hearty* heart-felt
22 *remorse* pity
24 *imprecations* prayers
27 *made* being
45 *overweighing* overruling

That this device may prove propitious,
And through the eyes and ears of Tamburlaine,
Convey events of mercy to his heart:
Grant that these signs of victory we yield   55
May bind the temples of his conquering head,
To hide the folded furrows of his brows,
And shadow his displeased countenance,
With happy looks of ruth and lenity.
Leave us my lord, and loving countrymen,   60
What simple virgins may persuade, we will.

GOVERNOR OF DAMASCUS
Farewell, sweet virgins, on whose safe return
Depends our city, liberty, and lives.

Exeunt [all except the VIRGINS]

Act V, Scene ii

[*Enter*] TAMBURLAINE, TECHELLES, THERIDAMAS, USUMCASANE,
with others: TAMBURLAINE *all in black, and very melancholy*

TAMBURLAINE
What are the turtles frayed out of their nests?
Alas poor fools, must you be first shall feel
The sworn destruction of Damascus?
They know my custom: could they not as well
Have sent ye out, when first my milk-white flags   5
Through which sweet mercy threw her gentle beams,
Reflexing them on your disdainful eyes:
As now when fury and incensed hate
Flings slaughtering terror from my coal-black tents,
And tells for truth, submissions comes too late?   10

FIRST VIRGIN
Most happy king and emperor of the earth,
Image of honour and nobility,
For whom the powers divine have made the world,
And on whose throne the holy Graces sit,
In whose sweet person is comprised the sum   15

---

54 *events* results   59 *ruth* pity
63 s.d. [*all except the* VIRGINS] ed. (O1 omits)
1 *turtles frayed* turtle-doves frightened
2 *fools* helpless ones
7 *Reflexing* reflecting

---

14 *Graces.* Three daughters of Jupiter, Euphrosyne, Aglaia, and Thalia,
the inspirers of all beauty.

Of nature's skill and heavenly majesty,
Pity our plights, O pity poor Damascus:
Pity old age, within whose silver hairs
Honour and reverence evermore have reigned,
Pity the marriage bed, where many a lord   20
In prime and glory of his loving joy
Embraceth now with tears of ruth and blood,
The jealous body of his fearful wife,
Whose cheeks and hearts so punished with conceit,
To think thy puissant never-stayed arm   25
Will part their bodies, and prevent their souls
From heavens of comfort yet their age might bear,
Now wax all pale and withered to the death,
As well for grief our ruthless governor
Have thus refused the mercy of thy hand   30
(Whose sceptre angels kiss, and Furies dread),
As for their liberties, their loves or lives.
O then for these, and such as we ourselves,
For us, for infants, and for all our bloods,
That never nourished thought against thy rule,   35
Pity, O pity, sacred emperor,
The prostrate service of this wretched town.
And take in sign thereof this gilded wreath,
Whereto each man of rule hath given his hand,
And wished as worthy subjects happy means,   40
To be investers of thy royal brows,
Even with the true Egyptian diadem.

TAMBURLAINE
Virgins, in vain ye labour to prevent
That which mine honour swears shall be performed:
Behold my sword, what see you at the point?   45

FIRST VIRGIN
Nothing but fear and fatal steel my lord.

TAMBURLAINE
Your fearful minds are thick and misty then,
For there sits Death, there sits imperious Death,
Keeping his circuit by the slicing edge.

23 *jealous* apprehensive
24 *punished with conceit* tormented by the thought
26–7 *prevent . . . From* deprive . . . of
46 s.p. ed. (Virg. O1)
49 *circuit* journey round a district (Death is likened to a judge)

31 *Furies.* See note on II, vii, 53 above.

But I am pleased you shall not see him there,   50
He now is seated on my horsemen's spears:
And on their points his fleshless body feeds.
Techelles, straight go charge a few of them
To charge these dames, and show my servant Death,
Sitting in scarlet on their armed spears.   55

VIRGINS
O pity us!

TAMBURLAINE
Away with them, I say, and show them Death.
                    [TECHELLES *and others*] *take them away*
I will not spare these proud Egyptians,
Nor charge my martial observations,
For all the wealth of Gihon's golden waves,   60
Or for the love of Venus, would she leave
The angry god of arms, and lie with me.
They have refused the offer of their lives,
And know my customs are as peremptory
As wrathful planets, death, or destiny.   65

                    Enter TECHELLES

What, have your horsemen shown the virgins Death?

TECHELLES
They have my lord, and on Damascus' walls
Have hoisted up their slaughtered carcasses.

TAMBURLAINE
A sight as baneful to their souls I think
As are Thessalian drugs or mithridate.   70
But go my lords, put the rest to the sword.
                    Exeunt [*all except* TAMBURLAINE]
Ah fair Zenocrate, divine Zenocrate,
Fair is too foul an epithet for thee,
That in thy passion for thy country's love,

55 *scarlet* (1) judge's robe, (2) blood
56 s.p. ed. (Omnes O1)
57 s.d. [TECHELLES *and others*] ed. (They O1)
59 *observations* customary practices
74 *passion* sorrow

60 *Gihon.* The second river of Eden (*Genesis* 2: 13).
62 *god of arms.* Mars, the lover of Venus.
70 *Thessalian.* Thessaly was traditionally regarded as the land of witch-craft.
70 *mithridate.* Here, apparently, poison. But generally mithridate was regarded as an antidote to poison.

And fear to see thy kingly father's harm,   75
With hair dishevelled wip'st thy watery cheeks:
And like to Flora in her morning's pride,
Shaking her silver tresses in the air,
Rain'st on earth resolved pearl in showers,
And sprinklest sapphires on thy shining face,   80
Where Beauty, mother to the Muses sits,
And comments volumes with her ivory pen:
Taking instructions from thy flowing eyes,
Eyes when that Ebena steps to heaven,
In silence of thy solemn evening walk,   85
Making the mantle of the richest night,
The moon, the planets, and the meteors, light.
There angels in their crystal armours fight
A doubtful battle with my tempted thoughts,
For Egypt's freedom and the Soldan's life: 90
His life that so consumes Zenocrate,
Whose sorrows lay more siege unto my soul,
Than all my army to Damascus' walls.
And neither Persians' sovereign, nor the Turk
Troubled my senses with conceit of foil,   95
So much by much, as doth Zenocrate.
What is beauty saith my sufferings then?
If all the pens that ever poets held,
Had fed the feeling of their masters' thoughts,
And every sweetness that inspired their hearts,   100
Their minds, and muses on admired themes:
If all the heavenly quintessence they still
From their immortal flowers of poesy,
Wherein as in a mirror we perceive
The highest reaches of a human wit—   105
If these had made one poem's period
And all combined in beauty's worthiness,

79 *resolved pearl* i.e., tears
91 *consumes* wastes with anxiety
95 *conceit of foil* idea of defeat
102 *quintessence* most essential part
102 *still* distil
105 *wit* imagination
106 *made . . . period* been combined to form a single poem in beauty's
     praise

77 *Flora.* The Roman goddess of springtime and flowers.
84 *Ebena.* No such deity is known.

Yet should there hover in their restless heads,
One thought, one grace, one wonder at the least,
Which into words no virtue can digest: 110
But how unseemly is it for my sex,
My discipline of arms and chivalry,
My nature and the terror of my name,
To harbour thoughts effeminate and faint.
Save only that in Beauty's just applause   115
With whose instinct the soul of man is touched,
And every warrior that is rapt with love,
Of fame, of valour, and of victory
Must need have beauty beat on his conceits,
I thus conceiving and subduing both   120
That which hath stopped the tempest of the gods,
Even from the fiery-spangled veil of heaven,
To feel the lovely warmth of shepherds' flames,
And march in cottages of strowed weeds,
Shall give the world to note for all my birth,   125
That virtue solely is the sum of glory,
And fashions men with true nobility.
Who's within there?

> *Enter two or three* [ATTENDANTS]

Hath Bajazeth been fed today?
ATTENDANT
Ay, my lord.   130

---

110 *Which . . . digest* which no power can express in words
114 *faint* weak
126 *virtue* the possession and display of manly qualities
126 *sum* the highest attainable point
130 s.p. ed. (An. O1)

115–27 *Save . . . nobility.* The most obscure passage in the text of the play, which unfortunately occurs at an important climax. Numerous emendations have been proposed. Professor Ellis-Fermor suggested that the printer of O1 might possibly have transposed the words 'that' and 'in' at l. 115, since reversing their order certainly gives a clearer sense. And G. I. Duthie (in 'The Dramatic Structure of Marlowe's *Tamburlaine the Great*, Parts I and II') would combine two emendations previously proposed for l. 121, making the line read 'That which hath stooped the topmost of the gods', a reference to Jove's wooing of Mnemosyme in the guise of a shepherd, which seems to be alluded to earlier in the play (I, ii, 199). But the general sense is clear enough: Tamburlaine, torn between love and honour, argues that the two can never be incompatible, since love of beauty provides the inspiration necessary to the heroism of the warrior.

TAMBURLAINE

Bring him forth, and let us know if the town be ransacked.

[Exeunt ATTENDANTS]

Enter TECHELLES, THERIDAMAS, USUMCASANE, *and others*

TECHELLES

The town is ours my lord, and fresh supply
Of conquest, and of spoil is offered us.

TAMBURLAINE

That's well Techelles, what's the news?

TECHELLES

The Soldan and the Arabian king together   135
March on us with such eager violence,
As if there were no way but one with us.

TAMBURLAINE

No more there is not, I warrant thee Techelles.

They bring in [BAJAZETH,] *the Turk* [*in his cage, followed by*
ZABINA]

THERIDAMAS

We know the victory is ours my lord,
But let us save the reverend Soldan's life,   140
For fair Zenocrate, that so laments his state.

TAMBURLAINE

That will we chiefly see unto, Theridamas.
For sweet Zenocrate, whose worthiness
Deserves a conquest over every heart:
And now, my footstool, if I lose the field,   145
You hope of liberty and restitution.
Here let him stay, my masters, from the tents,
Till we have made us ready for the field.
Pray for us Bajazeth, we are going.

Exeunt [*all except* BAJAZETH *and* ZABINA]

BAJAZETH

Go, never to return with victory: 150
Millions of men encompass thee about,
And gore thy body with as many wounds!
Sharp forked arrows light upon thy horse:
Furies from the black Cocytus lake,
Break up the earth, and with their firebrands,   155

149 s.d. [*all* . . . ZABINA] ed. (O1 omits)

---

154 *Furies.* See note to II, vii, 53 above.
154 *Cocytus.* Generally supposed to be a river in Hades. Here Marlowe refers
to it as a lake.

Enforce thee run upon the baneful pikes!
Volleys of shot pierce through thy charmed skin,
And every bullet dipped in poisoned drugs,
Or roaring cannons sever all thy joints,
Making thee mount as high as eagles soar!   160

ZABINA
Let all the swords and lances in the field,
Stick in his breast, as in their proper rooms,
At every pore let blood come dropping forth,
That lingering pains may massacre his heart,
And madness send his damned soul to hell!   165

BAJAZETH
Ah fair Zabina, we may curse his power,
The heavens may frown, the earth for anger quake,
But such a star hath influence in his sword,
As rules the skies, and countermands the gods,
More than Cimmerian Styx or destiny.   170
And then shall we in this detested guise,
With shame, with hunger, and with horror aye
Griping our bowels with retorqued thoughts,
And have no hope to end our ecstasies.

ZABINA
Then is there left no Mahomet, no God,   175
No fiend, no fortune, nor no hope of end
To our infamous monstrous slaveries?
Gape earth, and let the fiends infernal view
A hell, as hopeless and as full of fear
As are the blasted banks of Erebus: 180
Where shaking ghosts with ever-howling groans,
Hover about the ugly ferryman
To get a passage to Elysium.
Why should we live, O wretches, beggars, slaves,

156 *baneful* deadly
162 *proper rooms* appropriate places
172 *aye* forever
173 *retorqued* twisted back upon themselves
174 *ecstasies* frenzies
179 *A* ed. (As O1)
182–3 lineation ed.
183 *Elysium* ed. (Elisia O1)

---

170 *Cimmerian.* Black (see note at III, ii, 77 above).
180 *Erebus.* See note at IV, i, 45 above.
182 *ferryman.* Charon, who conveyed the souls of the dead across the river
    Styx.

Why live we Bajazeth, and build up nests,   185
So high within the region of the air,
By living long in this oppression,
That all the world will see and laugh to scorn
The former triumphs of our mightiness,
In this obscure infernal servitude?   190

BAJAZETH
O life more loathsome to my vexed thoughts,
Than noisome parbreak of the Stygian snakes,
Which fills the nooks of hell with standing air,
Infecting all the ghosts with cureless griefs:
O dreary engines of my loathed sight,   195
That sees my crown, my honour and my name,
Thrust under yoke and thraldom of a thief!
Why feed ye still on day's accursed beams,
And sink not quite into my tortured soul?
You see my wife, my queen and emperess,   200
Brought up and propped by the hand of fame,
Queen of fifteen contributory queens,
Now thrown to rooms of black abjection,
Smeared with blots of basest drudgery:
And villainess to shame, disdain, and misery: 205
Accursed Bajazeth, whose words of wrath,
That would with pity cheer Zabina's heart:
And make our souls resolve in ceaseless tears,
Sharp hunger bites upon and gripes the root:
From whence the issues of my thought do break.   210
O poor Zabina, O my queen, my queen,
Fetch me some water for my burning breast,
To cool and comfort me with longer date,
That in the shortened sequel of my life,
I may pour forth my soul into thine arms,   215
With words of love: whose moaning intercourse
Hath hitherto been stayed, with wrath and hate
Of our expressless banned inflictions.

192 *parbreak* vomit
193 *standing* stagnant
195 *engines* instruments
203 *abjection* degradation
205 *villainess* servant
208 *resolve* dissolve
213 *date* term of life
218 *expressless* inexpressible
218 *banned* cursed

ZABINA
> Sweet Bajazeth, I will prolong thy life,
> As long as any blood or spark of breath   220
> Can quench or cool the torments of my grief.

She goes out

BAJAZETH
> Now Bajazeth, abridge thy baneful days,
> And beat thy brains out of thy conquered head:
> Since other means are all forbidden me,
> That may be ministers of my decay.   225
> O highest lamp of ever-living Jove,
> Accursed day infected with my griefs,
> Hide now thy stained face in endless night,
> And shut the windows of the lightsome heavens.
> Let ugly Darkness with her rusty coach   230
> Engirt with tempests wrapped in pitchy clouds,
> Smother the earth with never-fading mists:
> And let her horses from their nostrils breathe
> Rebellious winds and dreadful thunderclaps:
> That in this terror Tamburlaine may live,   235
> And my pined soul resolved in liquid air,
> May still excruciate his tormented thoughts.
> Then let the strong dart of senseless cold,
> Pierce through the centre of my withered heart,
> And make a passage for my loathed life.   240

He brains himself against the cage

Enter ZABINA

ZABINA
> What do mine eyes behold, my husband dead?
> His skull all riven in twain, his brains dashed out?
> The brains of Bajazeth, my lord and sovereign?
> O Bajazeth, my husband and my lord,
> O Bajazeth, O Turk, O emperor, give him his liquor? Not I, 245
> bring milk and fire, and my blood I bring him again, tear me
> in pieces, give me the sword with a ball of wildfire upon it.
> Down with him, down with him! Go to my child, away,
> away, away! Ah, save that infant, save him, save him! I,
> even I speak to her, the sun was down. Streamers white, red, 250
> black, here, here, here! Fling the meat in his face. Tambur-
> laine, Tamburlaine, let the soldiers be buried. Hell, death,

225 *ministers . . . decay* instruments of death
236 *pined* tormented   236 *resolved* dissolved
236 *air* O3–4 (ay O1)   250 *Streamers* pennons

Tamburlaine, hell, make ready my coach, my chair, my
jewels, I come, I come, I come!
> *She runs against the cage and brains herself*

[*Enter*] ZENOCRATE *and* ANIPPE

ZENOCRATE

Wretched Zenocrate, that livest to see   255
Damascus' walls dyed with Egyptian blood,
Thy father's subjects and thy countrymen:
The streets strowed with disseevered joints of men,
And wounded bodies gasping yet for life.
But most accursed, to see the sun-bright troop   260
Of heavenly virgins and unspotted maids,
Whose looks might make the angry god of arms,
To break his sword and mildly treat of love,
On horsemen's lances to be hoisted up,
And guiltlessly endure a cruel death.   265
For every fell and stout Tartarian steed,
That stamped on others with their thundering hooves
When all their riders charged their quivering spears
Began to check the ground, and rein themselves:
Gazing upon the beauty of their looks: 270
Ah Tamburlaine, wert thou the cause of this
That term'st Zenocrate thy dearest love?
Whose lives were dearer to Zenocrate
Than her own life, or ought save thine own love.
But see another bloody spectacle!   275
Ah wretched eyes, the enemies of my heart,
How are ye glutted with these grievous objects,
And tell my soul more tales of bleeding ruth?
See, see Anippe if they breathe or no.

ANIPPE

No breath nor sense, nor motion in them both.   280
Ah madam, this their slavery hath enforced,
And ruthless cruelty of Tamburlaine.

ZENOCRATE

Earth cast up fountains from thy entrails,
And wet thy cheeks for their untimely deaths:

---

255 *Zenocrate* ed. (O1 omits; Zeno. O4)
266 *fell and stout* fierce and proud
268 *charged* levelled for the charge
269 *check the ground* paw the ground

---

262 *god of arms.* Mars.

Shake with their weight in sign of fear and grief: 285
Blush heaven, that gave them honour at their birth,
And let them die a death so barbarous,
Those that are proud of fickle empery,
And place their chiefest good in earthly pomp:
Behold the Turk and his great emperess.   290
Ah Tamburlaine, my love, sweet Tamburlaine,
That fights for sceptres and for slippery crowns,
Behold the Turk and his great emperess,
Thou that in conduct of thy happy stars,
Sleep'st every night with conquest on thy brows,   295
And yet wouldst shun the wavering turns of war.
In fear and feeling of the like distress,
Behold the Turk and his great emperess.
Ah mighty Jove and holy Mahomet,
Pardon my love, O pardon his contempt   300
Of earthly fortune, and respect of pity,
And let not conquest ruthlessly pursued
Be equally against his life incensed,
In this great Turk and hapless emperess.
And pardon me that was not moved with ruth,   305
To see them live so long in misery:
Ah what may chance to thee Zenocrate?

ANIPPE
Madam content yourself and be resolved,
Your love hath fortune so at his command,
That she shall stay and turn her wheel no more,   310
As long as life maintains his mighty arm,
That fights for honour to adorn your head.

Enter [PHILEMUS,] *a Messenger*

ZENOCRATE
What other heavy news now brings Philemus?

PHILEMUS
Madam, your father and th'Arabian king,
The first affecter of your excellence,   315
Comes now as Turnus 'gainst Aeneas did,

288 *empery* imperial rule
294 *in conduct* under the guidance   304 *In* as in
312 s.d. [PHILEMUS] ed. (O1 omits)
315 *affecter* lover

---

316 *Turnus.* The foe of Aeneas after Aeneas married Lavinia, formerly
betrothed to Turnus.

Armed with lance into the Egyptian fields,
Ready for battle 'gainst my lord the king.

ZENOCRATE

Now shame and duty, love and fear presents
A thousand sorrows to my martyred soul: 320
Whom should I wish the fatal victory,
When my poor pleasures are divided thus,
And racked by duty from my cursed heart?
My father and my first-betrothed love,
Must fight against my life and present love: 325
Wherein the change I use condemns my faith,
And makes my deeds infamous through the world.
But as the gods to end the Trojans' toil,
Prevented Turnus of Lavinia,
And fatally enriched Aeneas's love,   330
So for a final issue to my griefs,
To pacify my country and my love,
Must Tamburlaine by their resistless powers,
With virtue of a gentle victory,
Conclude a league of honour to my hope,   335
Then as the powers divine have preordained,
With happy safety of my father's life,
Send like defence of fair Arabia.

They sound to the battle. And TAMBURLAINE *enjoys the victory,
    after* [*which the* KING OF] ARABIA *enters wounded*

KING OF ARABIA

What cursed power guides the murdering hands,
Of this infamous tyrant's soldiers,   340
That no escape may save their enemies:
Nor fortune keep themselves from victory.
Lie down Arabia, wounded to the death,
And let Zenocrate's fair eyes behold
That as for her thou bear'st these wretched arms,   345
Even so for her thou diest in these arms:
Leaving thy blood for witness of thy love.

ZENOCRATE

Too dear a witness for such love my lord.
Behold Zenocrate, the cursed object
Whose fortunes never mastered her griefs: 350

326 *I use* I have effected
334 *With virtue . . . victory* in consequence of an honourable victory
335 *to* in accordance with
339 *murdering* ed. (murthering O1)

Behold her wounded in conceit for thee,
As much as thy fair body is for me.

KING OF ARABIA

Then shall I die with full contented heart,
Having beheld divine Zenocrate,
Whose sight with joy would take away my life,   355
As now it bringeth sweetness to my wound,
If I had not been wounded as I am.
Ah that the deadly pangs I suffer now,
Would lend an hour's licence to my tongue:
To make discourse of some sweet accidents   360
Have chanced thy merits in this worthless bondage.
And that I might be privy to the state,
Of thy deserved contentment and thy love:
But making now a virtue of thy sight,
To drive all sorrow from my fainting soul: 365
Since death denies me further cause of joy,
Deprived of care, my heart with comfort dies,
Since thy desired hand shall close mine eyes.

                                                    [*Dies*]

Enter TAMBURLAINE *leading in the* SOLDAN, TECHELLES,
        THERIDAMAS, USUMCASANE *with others*

TAMBURLAINE

Come happy father of Zenocrate,
A title higher than thy Soldan's name: 370
Though my right hand have thus enthralled thee,
Thy princely daughter here shall set thee free,
She that hath calmed the fury of my sword,
Which had ere this been bathed in streams of blood,
As vast and deep as Euphrates or Nile.   375

ZENOCRATE

O sight thrice welcome to my joyful soul,
To see the king my father issue safe,
From dangerous battle of my conquering love.

SOLDAN

Well met my only dear Zenocrate,
Though with the loss of Egypt and my crown.   380

TAMBURLAINE

'Twas I my lord that gat the victory,

351 *conceit* imagination
360 *sweet accidents* favourable occurrences
361 *Have* that have
378 *of* with

And therefore grieve not at your overthrow,
Since I shall render all into your hands,
And add more strength to your dominions
Than ever yet confirmed th'Egyptian crown.　　　　385
The god of war resigns his room to me,
Meaning to make me general of the world,
Jove viewing me in arms, looks pale and wan,
Fearing my power should pull him from his throne.
Where'er I come the Fatal Sisters sweat,　　　　390
And grisly Death by running to and fro,
To do their ceaseless homage to my sword:
And here in Afric where it seldom rains,
Since I arrived with my triumphant host,
Have swelling clouds drawn from wide gasping wounds,　　　　395
Been oft resolved in bloody purple showers,
A meteor that might terrify the earth,
And make it quake with every drop it drinks:
Millions of souls sit on the banks of Styx,
Waiting the back return of Charon's boat,　　　　400
Hell and Elysium swarm with ghosts of men,
That I have sent from sundry foughten fields,
To spread my fame through hell and up to heaven:
And see, my lord, a sight of strange import,
Emperors and kings lie breathless at my feet,　　　　405
The Turk and his great empress as it seems,
Left to themselves while we were at the fight,
Have desperately dispatched their slavish lives:
With them Arabia too hath left his life,
All sights of power to grace my victory:　　　　410
And such are objects fit for Tamburlaine,
Wherein as in a mirror may be seen
His honour, that consists in shedding blood,
When men presume to manage arms with him.

SOLDAN
Mighty hath God and Mahomet made thy hand,　　　　415
Renowned Tamburlaine, to whom all kings
Of force must yield their crowns and emperies,
And I am pleased with this my overthrow:
If as beseems a person of thy state,
Thou hast with honour used Zenocrate.　　　　420

385 *confirmed* established
401 *Elysium* ed. (Elesian O1)

390 *Fatal Sisters.* Fates (see note to I, ii, 174 above).

TAMBURLAINE
  Her state and person wants no pomp you see,
  And for all blot of foul inchastity,
  I record heaven, her heavenly self is clear:
  Then let me find no further time to grace
  Her princely temples with the Persian crown: 425
  But here these kings that on my fortunes wait:
  And have been crowned for proved worthiness,
  Even by this hand that shall establish them,
  Shall now, adjoining all their hands with mine,
  Invest her here my Queen of Persia.   430
  What saith the noble Soldan and Zenocrate?
SOLDAN
  I yield with thanks and protestations
  Of endless honour to thee for her love.
TAMBURLAINE
  Then doubt I not but fair Zenocrate
  Will soon consent to satisfy us both.   435
ZENOCRATE
  Else should I much forget myself, my lord.
THERIDAMAS
  Then let us set the crown upon her head,
  That hath long lingered for so high a seat.
TECHELLES
  My hand is ready to perform the deed,
  For now her marriage time shall work us rest.   440
USUMCASANE
  And here's the crown my lord, help set it on.
TAMBURLAINE
  Then sit thou down divine Zenocrate,
  And here we crown thee Queen of Persia,
  And all the kingdoms and dominions
  That late the power of Tamburlaine subdued: 445
  As Juno, when the giants were suppressed,
  That darted mountains at her brother Jove:
  So looks my love, shadowing in her brows
  Triumphs and trophies for my victories:
  Or as Latona's daughter bent to arms,   450
  Adding more courage to my conquering mind.

421 *wants* lack
433 *for her love* for your love of her
440 *work us* bring about for us

---

450 *Latona's daughter.* Artemis the huntress.

To gratify the sweet Zenocrate,
Egyptians, Moors, and men of Asia,
From Barbary unto the Western India,
Shall pay a yearly tribute to thy sire.   455
And from the bounds of Afric to the banks
Of Ganges, shall his mighty arm extend.
And now my lords and loving followers,
That purchased kingdoms by your martial deeds,
Cast off your armour, put on scarlet robes.   460
Mount up your royal places of estate,
Environed with troops of noblemen,
And there make laws to rule your provinces:
Hang up your weapons on Alcides' post,
For Tamburlaine takes truce with all the world.   465
Thy first betrothed love, Arabia,
Shall we with honour, as beseems, entomb,
With this great Turk and his fair emperess:
Then after all these solemn exequies,
We will our celebrated rites of marriage solemnize.   470

                                                              [*Exeunt*]

---

470 s.d. ed. (O1 omits)

464 *Alcides' post.* The doorpost of the temple of Hercules (Alcides).

Tamburlaine the Greate.

VVith his impaſsionate furie , for the
death of his Lady and Loue faire Zenocrate : his forme of exhortation and diſcipline
to his three Sonnes ,and the manner of
his owne death.

The ſecond part.

LONDON
Printed by E. A, *for* Ed. White, *and are to be ſolde*
at his Shop neere the little North doore of Saint Paules
Church at the Signe of the Gun.
1 6 0 6.

[DRAMATIS PERSONAE

TAMBURLAINE, *King of Persia*
CALYPHAS ⎫
AMYRAS ⎬ *his sons*
CELEBINUS ⎭
THERIDAMAS, *King of Argier*   5
TECHELLES, *King of Fez*
USUMCASANE, *King of Morocco*
ORCANES, *King of Natolia*
KING OF JERUSALEM
KING OF SORIA   10
KING OF TREBIZON
GAZELLUS, *Viceroy of Byron*
URIBASSA
SIGISMUND, *King of Hungary*
FREDERICK ⎫   15
BALDWIN ⎬ *peers of Hungary*
CALLAPINE, *son of Bajazeth and prisoner of Tamburlaine*
ALMEDA, *his keeper*
KING OF AMASIA
GOVERNOR OF BABYLON   20
CAPTAIN OF BALSERA
His SON
Another CAPTAIN
MAXIMUS
PERDICAS   25
LORDS, CITIZENS, SOLDIERS, PIONERS, PHYSICIANS, MESSENGERS, *and*
  ATTENDANTS

ZENOCRATE, *wife of Tamburlaine*
OLYMPIA, *wife of the Captain of Balsera*
Turkish CONCUBINES]   30

91

THE PROLOGUE

The general welcomes Tamburlaine received,
When he arrived last upon our stage,
Hath made our poet pen his second part,
Where death cuts off the progress of his pomp,
And murderous Fates throws all his triumphs down.   5
But what became of fair Zenocrate,
And with how many cities' sacrifice
He celebrated her sad funeral,
Himself in presence shall unfold at large.

8 *sad* ed. (said O1)

TAMBURLAINE THE GREAT

The Second Part of The Bloody Conquests of Mighty Tamburlaine. With his impassionate fury, for the death of his lady
and love, faire Zenocrate: his form of exhortation and discipline
to his three sons, and the manner of his own death.

Act I, Scene i

[*Enter*] ORCANES, KING OF NATOLIA; GAZELLUS, VICEROY OF
BYRON; URIBASSA, *and their train, with drums and trumpets*

ORCANES
    Egregious viceroys of these eastern parts,
    Placed by the issue of great Bajazeth,
    And sacred lord, the mighty Calapine:
    Who lives in Egypt, prisoner to that slave,
    Which kept his father in an iron cage: 5
    Now have we marched from fair Natolia
    Two hundred leagues, and on Danubius' banks,
    Our warlike host in complete armour rest,
    Where Sigismund the king of Hungary
    Should meet our person to conclude a truce.   10
    What? Shall we parle with the Christian,
    Or cross the stream, and meet him in the field?
GAZELLUS
    King of Natolia, let us treat of peace,
    We all are glutted with the Christians' blood,
    And have a greater foe to fight against,   15
    Proud Tamburlaine, that now in Asia,
    Near Guyron's head doth set his conquering feet,
    And means to fire Turkey as he goes:
    'Gainst him my lord must you address your power.

s.d. URIBASSA ed. (Upibassa O1)
1 *Egregious* distinguished
2 *issue* offspring
13 s.p. ed., here and throughout (Byr. O1)

---

6 *Natolia.* A more extensive area of Asia Minor than the present-day
Anatolia.
17 *Guyron.* Guiron, a town on the upper Euphrates, north-east of Aleppo.

URIBASSA

 Besides, King Sigismund hath brought from Christendom, 20
 More than his camp of stout Hungarians,
 Slavonians, Almains, Rutters, Muffs, and Danes,
 That with the halberd, lance, and murdering axe,
 Will hazard that we might with surety hold.

[ORCANES]

 Though from the shortest northern parallel, 25
 Vast Gruntland compassed with the frozen sea,
 Inhabited with tall and sturdy men,
 Giants as big as hugy Polypheme:
 Millions of soldiers cut the arctic line,
 Bringing the strength of Europe to these arms, 30
 Our Turkey blades shall glide through all their throats,
 And make this champion mead a bloody fen.
 Danubius' stream that runs to Trebizond,
 Shall carry wrapped within his scarlet waves,
 As martial presents to our friends at home 35
 The slaughtered bodies of these Christians.
 The Terrene main wherein Danubius falls,
 Shall by this battle be the bloody sea.

20 s.p. ed. (Upibassa O1)
22 *Slavonians* ed. (Sclavonians O1) Slavs
22 *Almains* ed. (Almans O1) Germans
22 *Rutters* horsemen
22 *Muffs* a derogatory term for Swiss or Germans
23 *halberd* a long-handled spear with an axe-edge
23 *murdering* ed. (murthering O1)
25 s.p. ed. (O1 omits) 26 *Gruntland* Greenland
26 *frozen sea* Arctic Ocean
32 *champion mead* level grassland

---

25 *shortest . . . parallel.* The smallest circle of latitude described on the
 globe toward the north.
27–8 *Inhabited . . . Giants.* A popular belief in Marlowe's day.
28 *Polypheme.* The Cyclops in Homer's *Odyssey.*
29 *cut . . . line.* Cross the Arctic Circle from the north.
33–41 'Marlowe sees the waters of the Danube sweeping from the river-
 mouths in two strong currents, the one racing across the Black Sea to
 Trebizond, the other swirling southward to the Bosphorus, and so
 onward to the Hellespont and the Aegean; both currents bear the
 slaughtered bodies of Christian soldiers, the one to bring proof of
 victory to the great Turkish town, the other to strike terror to the Italian
 merchants cruising round the Isles of Greece.' (E. Seaton, 'Marlowe's
 Map,' loc. cit., p. 33.)
37 *Terrene main.* The Mediterranean.

The wandering sailors of proud Italy,
Shall meet those Christians fleeting with the tide,   40
Beating in heaps against their argosies,
And make fair Europe mounted on her bull,
Trapped with the wealth and riches of the world,
Alight and wear a woeful mourning weed.

GAZELLUS

Yet stout Orcanes, prorex of the world,   45
Since Tamburlaine hath mustered all his men,
Marching from Cairo northward with his camp,
To Alexandria, and the frontier towns,
Meaning to make a conquest of our land:
'Tis requisite to parle for a peace   50
With Sigismund the king of Hungary:
And save our forces for the hot assaults
Proud Tamburlaine intends Natolia.

ORCANES

Viceroy of Byron, wisely hast thou said:
My realm, the centre of our empery   55
Once lost, all Turkey would be overthrown:
And for that cause the Christians shall have peace.
Slavonians, Almains, Rutters, Muffs, and Danes,
Fear not Orcanes, but great Tamburlaine,
Nor he, but Fortune that hath made him great.   60
We have revolted Grecians, Albanese,
Sicilians, Jews, Arabians, Turks, and Moors
Natolians, Sorians, black Egyptians,
Illyrians, Thracians, and Bithynians,
Enough to swallow forceless Sigismund   65
Yet scarce enough t'encounter Tamburlaine.
He brings a world of people to the field,

40 *fleeting* floating
41 *argosies* merchant ships
43 *Trapped* hung around
44 *weed* garment
45 *prorex* viceroy   47 *Cairo* ed. (Cairon O1)
55 *empery* empire
58 *Slavonians, Almains* see note to l. 22 above
59 *Fear* frighten   61 *Albanese* Albanians
63 *Sorians* Syrians
64 *Illyrians* O3-4 (Illicians O1)

---

42 *Europe . . . bull.* Zeus, in the form of a bull, carried Europa, the daughter
of Agenor, King of Phoenicia, across the sea to Crete.
54 *Byron.* A town near Babylon.

From Scythia to the oriental plage
Of India, where raging Lantchidol
Beats on the regions with his boisterous blows,   70
That never seaman yet discovered:
All Asia is in arms with Tamburlaine,
Even from the midst of fiery Cancer's tropic,
To Amazonia under Capricorn.
And thence as far as Archipelago,   75
All Afric is in arms with Tamburlaine.
Therefore viceroys the Christians must have peace.

Act I, Scene ii

[*Enter*] SIGISMUND, FREDERICK, BALDWIN, *and their train with*
drums and trumpets

SIGISMUND

Orcanes, as our legates promised thee,
We with our peers have crossed Danubius' stream
To treat of friendly peace or deadly war:
Take which thou wilt, for as the Romans used,
I here present thee with a naked sword.   5
Wilt thou have war, then shake this blade at me,
If peace, restore it to my hands again:
And I will sheathe it to confirm the same.

ORCANES

Stay Sigismund, forgett'st thou I am he
That with the cannon shook Vienna walls,   10
And made it dance upon the continent:
As when the massy substance of the earth
Quiver about the axle-tree of heaven?
Forgett'st thou that I sent a shower of darts,
Mingled with powdered shot and feathered steel,   15
So thick upon the blink-eyed burghers' heads,
That thou thyself, then County Palatine,

68 *oriental plage* eastern shore
69 *Lantchidol* an arm of the Indian Ocean
75 *thence . . . Archipelago* northward to the Mediterranean islands
13 *axle-tree of heaven* see note to Part One, IV, ii, 50 above
16 *blink-eyed* unable to look steadily upon the missiles
17 *County* Count

73–4 *from . . . Capricorn.* i.e., from the Canaries, the centre of the Tropic
of Cancer, to the region known as Amazonia, near the supposed sources
of the Nile.

The King of Boheme, and the Austric Duke,
Sent heralds out, which basely on their knees
In all your names desired a truce of me?   20
Forgett'st thou, that to have me raise my siege,
Wagons of gold were set before my tent:
Stamped with the princely fowl that in her wings
Carries the fearful thunderbolts of Jove?
How canst thou think of this and offer war?   25

SIGISMUND

Vienna was besieged, and I was there,
Then County Palatine, but now a king:
And what we did was in extremity:
But now Orcanes, view my royal host,
That hides these plains, and seems as vast and wide,   30
As doth the desert of Arabia
To those that stand on Badgeth's lofty tower,
Or as the ocean to the traveller
That rests upon the snowy Appenines:
And tell me whether I should stoop so low,   35
Or treat of peace with the Natolian king?

GAZELLUS

Kings of Natolia and of Hungary,
We came from Turkey to confirm a league,
And not to dare each other to the field:
A friendly parle might become ye both.   40

FREDERICK

And we from Europe to the same intent,
Which if your general refuse or scorn,
Our tents are pitched, our men stand in array,
Ready to charge you ere you stir your feet.

ORCANES

So prest are we, but yet if Sigismund   45
Speak as a friend, and stand not upon terms,
Here is his sword, let peace be ratified
On these conditions specified before,
Drawn with advice of our ambassadors.

SIGISMUND

Then here I sheathe it, and give thee my hand,   50
Never to draw it out, or manage arms
Against thyself or thy confederates:
But whilst I live will be at truce with thee.

18 *Austric* Austrian   23 *princely fowl* the eagle
32 *Badgeth* Bagdad
45 s.p. ed. and so throughout (Nat. O1)   45 *prest* ready

ORCANES
But, Sigismund, confirm it with an oath,
And swear in sight of heaven and by thy Christ.   55

SIGISMUND
By Him that made the world and saved my soul,
The Son of God and issue of a maid,
Sweet Jesus Christ, I solemnly protest,
And vow to keep this peace inviolable.

ORCANES
By sacred Mahomet, the friend of God,   60
Whose holy Alcoran remains with us,
Whose glorious body when he left the world,
Closed in a coffin mounted up the air,
And hung on stately Mecca's temple roof,
I swear to keep this truce inviolable: 65
Of whose conditions, and our solemn oaths
Signed with our hands, each shall retain a scroll:
As memorable witness of our league.
Now Sigismund, if any Christian king
Encroach upon the confines of thy realm,   70
Send word, Orcanes of Natolia
Confirmed this league beyond Danubius' stream,
And they will, trembling, sound a quick retreat,
So am I feared among all nations.

SIGISMUND
If any heathen potentate or king   75
Invade Natolia, Sigismund will send
A hundred thousand horse trained to the war,
And backed by stout lancers of Germany,
The strength and sinews of the imperial seat.

ORCANES
I thank thee Sigismund, but when I war   80
All Asia Minor, Africa, and Greece
Follow my standard and my thundering drums:
Come let us go and banquet in our tents:
I will dispatch chief of my army hence
To fair Natolia, and to Trebizon,   85
To stay my coming 'gainst proud Tamburlaine.
Friend Sigismund, and peers of Hungary,
Come banquet and carouse with us a while,
And then depart we to our territories.   *Exeunt*

70 *confines* borders
84 *chief* most
86 *stay* await

Act I, Scene iii

[Enter] CALLAPINE *with* ALMEDA, *his keeper*

CALLAPINE
Sweet Almeda, pity the ruthful plight
Of Callapine, the son of Bajazeth,
Born to be monarch of the western world:
Yet here detained by cruel Tamburlaine.

ALMEDA
My lord I pity it, and with my heart
Wish your release, but he whose wrath is death,
My sovereign lord, renowned Tamburlaine,
Forbids you further liberty than this.

CALLAPINE
Ah were I now but half so eloquent
To paint in words, what I'll perform in deeds,   10
I know thou wouldst depart from hence with me.

ALMEDA
Not for all Afric, therefore move me not.

CALLAPINE
Yet hear me speak, my gentle Almeda.

ALMEDA
No speech to that end, by your favour sir.

CALLAPINE
By Cairo runs—   15

ALMEDA
No talk of running, I tell you sir.

CALLAPINE
A little further, gentle Almeda.

ALMEDA
Well sir, what of this?

CALLAPINE
By Cairo runs to Alexandria bay,
Darote's streams, wherein at anchor lies   20
A Turkish galley of my royal fleet,
Waiting my coming to the river side,
Hoping by some means I shall be released,

3 *western world* Turkish empire
12 *move* urge
15 *Cairo* ed. and so throughout (Cario O1)

20 *Darote's streams.* The Nile from Cairo to Alexandria, which runs by the
town of Darote.

Which when I come aboard will hoist up sail,
And soon put forth into the Terrene sea: 25
Where 'twixt the isles of Cyprus and of Crete,
We quickly may in Turkish seas arrive.
Then shalt thou see a hundred kings and more
Upon their knees, all bid me welcome home.
Amongst so many crowns of burnished gold,   30
Choose which thou wilt, all are at thy command,
A thousand galleys manned with Christian slaves
I freely give thee, which shall cut the straits,
And bring armadoes from the coast of Spain,
Fraughted with gold of rich America: 35
The Grecian virgins shall attend on thee,
Skilful in music and in amorous lays:
As fair as was Pygmalion's ivory girl,
Or lovely Iö metamorphosed.
With naked negroes shall thy coach be drawn,   40
And as thou rid'st in triumph through the streets,
The pavement underneath thy chariot wheels
With Turkey carpets shall be covered:
And cloth of Arras hung about the walls,
Fit objects for thy princely eye to pierce.   45
A hundred bassoes clothed in crimson silk
Shall ride before thee on Barbarian steeds:
And when thou goest, a golden canopy
Enchased with precious stones, which shine as bright
As that fair veil that covers all the world: 50
When Phoebus leaping from his hemisphere,
Descendeth downward to th'antipodes.
And more than this, for all I cannot tell.

34 *armadoes* warships
35 *Fraughted* laden
44 *cloth of Arras* rich tapestry fabric
46 *bassoes* bashaws
48 *goest* walk
49 *Enchased* adorned
51 *Phoebus* the sun

38 *Pygmalion's ivory girl* Galatea, the statue created by the sculptor Pygmalion and brought to life by Aphrodite.
39 *Iö*. Daughter of Inachus, King of Argos. She was loved by Zeus and transformed into a heifer through his fear of Hera.
52 *Antipodes*. A group of islands in the western Pacific, amongst which the sun was believed to set.

ALMEDA
How far hence lies the galley, say you?
CALLAPINE
Sweet Almeda, scarce half a league from hence.   55
ALMEDA
But need we not be spied going aboard?
CALLAPINE
Betwixt the hollow hanging of a hill
And crooked bending of a craggy rock,
The sails wrapped up, the mast and tacklings down,
She lies so close that none can find her out.   60
ALMEDA
I like that well: but tell me my lord, if I should let you go,
would you be as good as your word? Shall I be made a king
for my labour?
CALLAPINE
As I am Callapine the emperor,
And by the hand of Mahomet I swear,   65
Thou shalt be crowned a king and be my mate.
ALMEDA
Then here I swear, as I am Almeda,
Your keeper under Tamburlaine the Great
(For that's the style and title I have yet),
Although he sent a thousand armed men   70
To intercept this haughty enterprize,
Yet would I venture to conduct your grace,
And die before I brought you back again.
CALLAPINE
Thanks gentle Almeda, then let us haste,
Lest time be past and lingering let us both.   75
ALMEDA
When you will my lord, I am ready.
CALLAPINE
Even straight: and farewell cursed Tamburlaine.
Now go I to revenge my father's death.   *Exeunt*

56 *need we not* shall we not inevitably
60 *close* concealed
66 *mate* equal
69 *style* designation
75 *let* hinder
77 *straight* immediately

Act I, Scene iv

[*Enter*] TAMBURLAINE *with* ZENOCRATE, *and his three sons,*
CALYPHAS, AMYRAS, *and* CELEBINUS, *with drums and trumpets*

TAMBURLAINE
Now, bright Zenocrate, the world's fair eye,
Whose beams illuminate the lamps of heaven,
Whose cheerful looks do clear the cloudy air
And clothe it in a crystal livery,
Now rest thee here on fair Larissa plains   5
Where Egypt and the Turkish empire parts,
Between thy sons that shall be emperors,
And every one commander of a world.

ZENOCRATE
Sweet Tamburlaine, when wilt thou leave these arms
And save thy sacred person free from scathe,   10
And dangerous chances of the wrathful war?

TAMBURLAINE
When heaven shall cease to move on both the poles
And when the ground whereon my soldiers march
Shall rise aloft and touch the horned moon,
And not before, my sweet Zenocrate: 15
Sit up and rest thee like a lovely queen.
So, now she sits in pomp and majesty:
When these my sons, more precious in mine eyes
Than all the wealthy kingdoms I subdued,
Placed by her side, look on their mother's face.   20
But yet methinks their looks are amorous,
Not martial as the sons of Tamburlaine.
Water and air being symbolized in one
Argue their want of courage and of wit,
Their hair as white as milk and soft as down,   25
Which should be like the quills of porcupines,
As black as jet, and hard as iron or steel,
Bewrays they are too dainty for the wars.
Their fingers made to quaver on a lute,

18 *precious* ed. (procions O1)
21 *amorous* loving, gentle
28 *Bewrays* betrays, reveals

---

5 *Larissa*. A sea-coast town south of Gaza, the present-day El Arish.
23–4 *Water ... wit*. Being overbalanced in the phlegmatic and sanguine
   humours (water and blood), the boys lack the bile and choler which
   might give them courage and wit.

Their arms to hang about a lady's neck: 30
Their legs to dance and caper in the air:
Would make me think them bastards, not my sons,
But that I know they issued from thy womb,
That never looked on man but Tamburlaine.

ZENOCRATE

My gracious lord, they have their mother's looks,   35
But when they list, their conquering father's heart:
This lovely boy, the youngest of the three,
Not long ago bestrid a Scythian steed:
Trotting the ring and tilting at a glove:
Which when he tainted with his slender rod,   40
He reined him straight and made him so curvet,
As I cried out for fear he should have fallen.

TAMBURLAINE

Well done my boy, thou shalt have shield and lance,
Armour of proof, horse, helm, and curtle-axe,
And I will teach thee how to charge thy foe,   45
And harmless run among the deadly pikes.
If thou wilt love the wars and follow me,
Thou shalt be made a king and reign with me,
Keeping in iron cages emperors.
If thou exceed thy elder brothers' worth,   50
And shine in complete virtue more than they,
Thou shalt be king before them, and thy seed
Shall issue crowned from their mother's womb.

CELEBINUS

Yes father, you shall see me if I live,
Have under me as many kings as you,   55
And march with such a multitude of men,
As all the world shall tremble at their view.

TAMBURLAINE

These words assure me boy, thou art my son.
When I am old and cannot manage arms,
Be thou the scourge and terror of the world.   60

AMYRAS

Why may not I my lord, as well as he,
Be termed the scourge and terror of the world?

36 *list* wish, choose
40 *tainted* struck (a technical term in tilting)
44 *proof* tested strength
44 *curtle-axe* heavy slashing sword
51 *virtue* manly qualities

TAMBURLAINE

Be all a scourge and terror to the world,
Or else you are not sons of Tamburlaine.

CALYPHAS

But while my brothers follow arms my lord,   65
Let me accompany my gracious mother,
They are enough to conquer all the world
And you have won enough for me to keep.

TAMBURLAINE

Bastardly boy, sprung from some coward's loins,
And not the issue of great Tamburlaine,   70
Of all the provinces I have subdued
Thou shalt not have a foot, unless thou bear
A mind courageous and invincible:
For he shall wear the crown of Persia,
Whose head hath deepest scars, whose breast most wounds,   75
Which being wroth, sends lightning from his eyes,
And in the furrows of his frowning brows,
Harbours revenge, war, death and cruelty:
For in a field whose superficies
Is covered with a liquid purple veil,   80
And sprinkled with the brains of slaughtered men,
My royal chair of state shall be advanced:
And he that means to place himself therein
Must armed wade up to his chin in blood.

ZENOCRATE

My lord, such speeches to our princely sons,   85
Dismays their minds before they come to prove
The wounding troubles angry war affords.

CELEBINUS

No madam, these are speeches fit for us,
For if his chair were in a sea of blood,
I would prepare a ship and sail to it,   90
Ere I would lose the title of a king.

AMYRAS

And I would strive to swim through pools of blood,
Or make a bridge of murdered carcasses,
Whose arches should be framed with bones of Turks,
Ere I would lose the title of a king.   95

TAMBURLAINE

Well lovely boys, you shall be emperors both,

79 *superficies* ed. (superfluities O1) surface
86 *prove* find out by experience
93 *murdered* ed. (murthered O1)

Stretching your conquering arms from east to west:
And sirrah, if you mean to wear a crown,
When we shall meet the Turkish deputy
And all his viceroys, snatch it from his head,   100
And cleave his pericranion with thy sword.

CALYPHAS
If any man will hold him, I will strike,
And cleave him to the channel with my sword.

TAMBURLAINE
Hold him and cleave him too, or I'll cleave thee,
For we will march against them presently.   105
Theridamas, Techelles, and Casane
Promised to meet me on Larissa plains
With hosts apiece against this Turkish crew,
For I have sworn by sacred Mahomet,
To make it parcel of my empery.   110
The trumpets sound Zenocrate, they come.

Act I, Scene v

Enter THERIDAMAS *and his train with drums and trumpets*

TAMBURLAINE
Welcome Theridamas, King of Argier.

THERIDAMAS
My lord the great and mighty Tamburlaine,
Arch-monarch of the world, I offer here
My crown, myself, and all the power I have,
In all affection at thy kingly feet.   5

TAMBURLAINE
Thanks good Theridamas.

THERIDAMAS
Under my colours march ten thousand Greeks,
And of Argier and Afric's frontier towns,
Twice twenty thousand valiant men-at-arms,
All which have sworn to sack Natolia: 10
Five hundred brigandines are under sail,
Meet for your service on the sea, my lord,

---

101 *pericranion* skull
103 *channel* the channel-bone, or collar-bone
110 *parcel . . . empery* part of my empire
  8 *Argier* Algiers
 11 *brigandines* brigantines, small vessels which could be either
    sailed or rowed

That launching from Argier to Tripoly,
Will quickly ride before Natolia:
And batter down the castles on the shore.   15
TAMBURLAINE
Well said Argier, receive thy crown again.

Act I, Scene vi

Enter TECHELLES *and* USUMCASANE *together*

TAMBURLAINE
Kings of Morocco and of Fez, welcome.
USUMCASANE
Magnificent and peerless Tamburlaine,
I and my neighbour King of Fez have brought
To aid thee in this Turkish expedition,
A hundred thousand expert soldiers: 5
From Azamor to Tunis near the sea,
Is Barbary unpeopled for thy sake,
And all the men in armour under me,
Which with my crown I gladly offer thee.
TAMBURLAINE
Thanks King of Morocco, take your crown again.   10
TECHELLES
And mighty Tamburlaine, our earthly god,
Whose looks make this inferior world to quake,
I here present thee with the crown of Fez,
And with an host of Moors trained to the war,
Whose coal-black faces make their foes retire,   15
And quake for fear, as if infernal Jove,
Meaning to aid thee in these Turkish arms,
Should pierce the black circumference of hell,
With ugly furies bearing fiery flags,
And millions of his strong tormenting spirits: 20
From strong Tesella unto Biledull,
All Barbary is unpeopled for thy sake.

1 *Morocco* ed., and so throughout (Moroccus O1)
1 *Fez* ed., and so throughout (Fesse O1)
17 *thee* ed. (them O1)
17 *these* O3–4 (this O1)

---

6 *Azamor*. A town in North Africa.
16 *infernal Jove*. Pluto. The Furies were in his service.
21 *Tesella . . . Biledull*. A town and a province in North Africa.

TAMBURLAINE

Thanks King of Fez, take here thy crown again.
Your presence, loving friends and fellow kings,
Makes me to surfeit in conceiving joy;   25
If all the crystal gates of Jove's high court
Were opened wide, and I might enter in
To see the state and majesty of heaven,
It could not more delight me than your sight.
Now will we banquet on these plains a while,   30
And after march to Turkey with our camp,
In numbers more than are the drops that fall
When Boreas vents a thousand swelling clouds.
And proud Orcanes of Natolia,
With all his viceroys shall be so afraid,   35
That though the stones, as at Deucalion's flood,
Were turned to men, he should be overcome:
Such lavish will I make of Turkish blood,
That Jove shall send his winged messenger
To bid me sheathe my sword, and leave the field: 40
The sun unable to sustain the sight,
Shall hide his head in Thetis' watery lap
And leave his steeds to fair Boötes' charge:
For half the world shall perish in this fight;
But now my friends, let me examine ye,   45
How have ye spent your absent time from me?

USUMCASANE

My lord our men of Barbary have marched
Four hundred miles with armour on their backs,
And lain in leaguer fifteen months and more,
For since we left you at the Soldan's court,   50
We have subdued the southern Guallatia,
And all the land unto the coast of Spain.

33 *Boreas* the north wind
38 *lavish* spilling, squandering
43 *Boötes* O3–4 (Boetes O1). See note to Part One, I, ii, 207 above
49 *in leaguer* in camp

36–7 *stones … men.* Deucalion and his wife Pyrrha were the sole survivors of a flood sent by Zeus to exterminate the human race. They
   repopulated the earth by casting stones to the earth, from which
   sprang men and women.
39 *winged messenger.* Mercury.
42 *Thetis.* A sea goddess.
51 *Guallatia.* Gualata, a province in North Africa, south-west of the
   Sahara.

We kept the narrow Strait of Gibraltar,
And made Canaria call us kings and lords,
Yet never did they recreate themselves,   55
Or cease one day from war and hot alarms,
And therefore let them rest a while my lord.

TAMBURLAINE
They shall Casane, and 'tis time i'faith.

TECHELLES
And I have marched along the river Nile,
To Machda, where the mighty Christian priest   60
Called John the Great, sits in a milk-white robe,
Whose triple mitre I did take by force,
And made him swear obedience to my crown.
From thence unto Cazates did I march,
Where Amazonians met me in the field: 65
With whom (being women) I vouchsafed a league,
And with my power did march to Zanzibar,
The western part of Afric, where I viewed
The Ethiopian sea, rivers and lakes:
But neither man nor child in all the land: 70
Therefore I took my course to Manico,
Where unresisted I removed my camp:
And by the coast of Byather at last,
I came to Cubar, where the negroes dwell,
And conquering that, made haste to Nubia,   75
There having sacked Borno the kingly seat,

---

54 *Canaria*. The Canary Islands.
59–78 *And ... before*. Earlier criticisms of Marlowe's geography were
   answered by Miss Ethel Seaton in her article 'Marlowe's Map', where
   she demonstrated that the campaigns of Techelles can actually be
   followed on the maps of Ortelius. Techelles' march covered a very
   large part of the continent of Africa.
60 *Machda*. An Abyssinian town on a tributary of the Nile.
61 *John the Great*. Prester (or Presbiter) John, the legendary priest-king
   supposed to rule a vast Asiatic empire.
64 *Cazates*. A town in *Amazonium regio* (the territory west of Mozambique
   in Ortelius) where the Nile rises out of Lake Victoria.
65 *Amazonians*. Warlike women, supposed to inhabit *Amazonium regio*.
67 *Zanzibar*. The west coast of Africa in Ortelius.
69 *Ethiopian sea*. The name given in Ortelius to the ocean separating the
   west coast of Africa from South America.
71 *Manico*. Manicongo.
73 *Byather*. Biafar.
74 *Cubar*. Gubar, the chief town of Biafar.
76 *Borno*. The chief town of Nubia.

I took the king, and led him bound in chains
Unto Damascus, where I stayed before.

TAMBURLAINE
Well done Techelles: what saith Theridamas?

THERIDAMAS
I left the confines and the bounds of Afric   80
And made a voyage into Europe,
Where by the river Tyros I subdued
Stoka, Padalia, and Codemia.
Then crossed the sea and came to Oblia,
And Nigra Silva, where the devils dance,   85
Which in despite of them I set on fire:
From thence I crossed the gulf, called by the name
Mare Majore of th'inhabitants:
Yet shall my soldiers make no period
Until Natolia kneel before your feet.   90

TAMBURLAINE
Then will we triumph, banquet and carouse,
Cooks shall have pensions to provide us cates,
And glut us with the dainties of the world,
Lachryma Christi and Calabrian wines
Shall common soldiers drink in quaffing bowls,   95
Ay, liquid gold when we have conquered him,
Mingled with coral and with orient pearl:
Come let us banquet and carouse the whiles.

                                        Exeunt

78 *Damascus* ed., and so throughout (Damasco O1)
89 *period* pause
92 *cates* delicacies
94 *Lachryma Christi* a sweet wine of southern Italy
97 *orient* ed. (orientall O1) lustrous

80–90 *I left . . . feet*. The campaign of Theridamas can also be traced on
  Ortelius' maps. (See Seaton, p. 29.)
82 *river Tyros*. The Dniester, forming the southern boundary of the
  province of Podolia (or Padalia) north-west of the Black Sea.
83 *Stoka*. A town on the river Dniester.
  Codemia. A town north-east of Stoka.
84 *Oblia*. Olbia, a town separated from Codemia by the *Nigra Silva*
  (Black Forest).
88 *Mare Majore*. The Black Sea.

Act II, Scene i

[Enter] SIGISMUND, FREDERICK, BALDWIN, *with their train*

SIGISMUND
Now say my lords of Buda and Bohemia,
What motion is it that inflames your thoughts,
And stirs your valours to such sudden arms?

FREDERICK
Your majesty remembers, I am sure,
What cruel slaughter of our Christian bloods,   5
These heathenish Turks and pagans lately made,
Betwixt the city Zula and Danubius,
How through the midst of Varna and Bulgaria
And almost to the very walls of Rome,
They have not long since massacred our camp.   10
It resteth now then that your majesty
Take all advantages of time and power,
And work revenge upon these infidels:
Your highness knows, for Tamburlaine's repair,
That strikes a terror to all Turkish hearts.   15
Natolia hath dismissed the greatest part
Of all his army, pitched against our power
Betwixt Cutheia and Orminius' mount,
And sent them marching up to Belgasar,
Acantha, Antioch, and Caesarea,   20
To aid the kings of Soria and Jerusalem.
Now then my lord, advantage take hereof,
And issue suddenly upon the rest:
That in the fortune of their overthrow,
We may discourage all the pagan troop,   25
That dare attempt to war with Christians.

2 *motion* emotion
8 *Varna* ed. (Verna O1)
11 *resteth* remains
14 *repair* arrival

---

1 *Buda.* A city on the Danube, now part of Budapest.
7 *Zula.* A town which Ortelius locates north of the Danube.
8 *Varna.* A city in north-east Bulgaria.
9 *Rome.* Possibly Constantinople. (See Seaton, p. 30.)
18 *Cutheia.* Chiutaie, a town and district in Anatolia.
Orminius' mount. Mt Horminius in Bithynia.
19 *Belgasar.* Belglasar, a town east of Chiutaie.
20 *Acantha.* Acanta, a town south-east of Belglasar.

SIGISMUND

But calls not then your grace to memory
The league we lately made with King Orcanes,
Confirmed by oaths and articles of peace,
And calling Christ for record of our truths?　　　30
This should be treachery and violence,
Against the grace of our profession.

BALDWIN

No whit my lord: for with such infidels,
In whom no faith nor true religion rests,
We are not bound to those accomplishments,　　　35
The holy laws of Christendom enjoin:
But as the faith which they profanely plight
Is not by necessary policy,
To be esteemed assurance for ourselves,
So what we vow to them should not infringe　　　40
Our liberty of arms and victory.

SIGISMUND

Though I confess the oaths they undertake,
Breed little strength to our security,
Yet those infirmities that thus defame
Their faiths, their honours, and their religion,　　　45
Should not give us presumption to the like.
Our faiths are sound, and must be consummate,
Religious, righteous, and inviolate.

FREDERICK

Assure your grace 'tis superstition
To stand so strictly on dispensive faith:　　　50
And should we lose the opportunity
That God hath given to venge our Christians' death
And scourge their foul blasphemous paganism,
As fell to Saul, to Balaam, and the rest,
That would not kill and curse at God's command,　　　55
So surely will the vengeance of the Highest

33 *No whit* not in the least
35 *accomplishments* performance of obligation
37 *plight* pledge themselves to
47 *consummate* ed. (consinuate O1) perfect
50 *dispensive faith* oath which may be set aside by dispensation

54 *Saul . . . Balaam.* Saul failed to kill King Agag and his flocks (I *Samuel* 15), but Balaam obeyed God in refusing to curse the children of Israel (*Numbers*, 22–4); so Frederick's appeal to scriptural authority is confused.

And jealous anger of His fearful arm
Be poured with rigour on our sinful heads,
If we neglect this offered victory.

SIGISMUND

Then arm, my lords, and issue suddenly,   60
Giving commandment to our general host,
With expedition to assail the pagan,
And take the victory our God hath given.   *Exeunt*

Act II, Scene ii

[*Enter*] ORCANES, GAZELLUS, URIBASSA, *with their train*

ORCANES

Gazellus, Uribassa, and the rest,
Now will we march from proud Orminius' mount
To fair Natolia, where our neighbour kings
Expect our power and our royal presence,
T'encounter with the cruel Tamburlaine,   5
That nigh Larissa sways a mighty host,
And with the thunder of his martial tools
Makes earthquakes in the hearts of men and heaven.

GAZELLUS

And now come we to make his sinews shake,
With greater power than erst his pride hath felt,   10
An hundred kings by scores will bid him arms,
An hundred thousand subjects to each score:
Which if a shower of wounding thunderbolts
Should break out of the bowels of the clouds
And fall as thick as hail upon our heads,   15
In partial aid of the proud Scythian,
Yet should our courages and steeled crests,
And numbers more than infinite of men,
Be able to withstand and conquer him.

URIBASSA

Methinks I see how glad the Christian king   20
Is made, for joy of your admitted truce:
That could not but before be terrified:
With unacquainted power of our host.

Enter a MESSENGER

62 *expedition* speed
7 *martial tools* military equipment   10 *erst* hitherto
11 *bid him arms* challenge him to fight
16 *partial* biased, prejudiced

MESSENGER

  Arm, dread sovereign and my noble lords!

  The treacherous army of the Christians,   25

  Taking advantage of your slender power,

  Comes marching on us, and determines straight,

  To bid us battle for our dearest lives.

ORCANES

  Traitors, villains, damned Christians!

  Have I not here the articles of peace,   30

  And solemn covenants we have both confirmed,

  He by his Christ, and I by Mahomet?

GAZELLUS

  Hell and confusion light upon their heads,

  That with such treason seek our overthrow,

  And cares so little for their prophet Christ!   35

ORCANES

  Can there be such deceit in Christians,

  Or treason in the fleshly heart of man,

  Whose shape is figure of the highest God?

  Then if there be a Christ, as Christians say,

  But in their deeds deny him for their Christ: 40

  If he be son to everlasting Jove,

  And hath the power of his outstretched arm,

  If he be jealous of his name and honour,

  As is our holy prophet Mahomet,

  Take here these papers as our sacrifice   45

  And witness of thy servant's perjury.

  Open, thou shining veil of Cynthia

  And make a passage from the empyreal heaven

  That He that sits on high and never sleeps,

  Nor in one place is circumscriptible,   50

  But everywhere fills every continent,

  With strange infusion of His sacred vigour,

  May in His endless power and purity

  Behold and venge this traitor's perjury.

  Thou Christ that art esteemed omnipotent,   55

  If thou wilt prove thyself a perfect God,

  Worthy the worship of all faithful hearts,

  Be now revenged upon this traitor's soul,

  And make the power I have left behind

  (Too little to defend our guiltless lives)   60

38 *figure* image
47 *Cynthia* the moon
48 *empyreal* ed. (imperial O1)

Sufficient to discomfort and confound
The trustless force of these false Christians.
To arms, my lords, on Christ still let us cry:
If there be Christ, we shall have victory.   [*Exeunt*]

Act II, Scene iii

Sound to the battle, and SIGISMUND *comes out wounded*

SIGISMUND

Discomfited is all the Christian host,
And God hath thundered vengeance from on high,
For my accursed and hateful perjury.
O just and dreadful punisher of sin,
Let the dishonour of the pains I feel,   5
In this my mortal well-deserved wound,
End all my penance in my sudden death,
And let this death wherein to sin I die,
Conceive a second life in endless mercy!   [*Dies*]

Enter ORCANES, GAZELLUS, URIBASSA, *with others*

ORCANES

Now lie the Christians bathing in their bloods,   10
And Christ or Mahomet hath been my friend.

GAZELLUS

See here the perjured traitor Hungary,
Bloody and breathless for his villainy.

ORCANES

Now shall his barbarous body be a prey
To beasts and fowls, and all the winds shall breathe   15
Through shady leaves of every senseless tree,
Murmurs and hisses for his heinous sin.
Now scalds his soul in the Tartarian streams,
And feeds upon the baneful tree of hell,
That Zoacum, that fruit of bitterness,   20

64 s.d. ed. (O1 omits)
 1 *Discomfited* routed
 8 *wherein . . . die* which absolves me from my sin
 9 s.d. ed. (O1 omits)   16 *senseless* unfeeling

18 *Tartarian.* Of Tartarus, the region of hell where the worst sinners were
   punished.
20 *Zoacum* (or *Ezecum*). A tree of hell described in the Koran, XXXVII,
   60–4.

That in the midst of fire is ingraft,
Yet flourisheth as Flora in her pride,
With apples like the heads of damned fiends,
The devils there in chains of quenchless flame,
Shall lead his soul through Orcus' burning gulf: 25
From pain to pain, whose change shall never end:
What sayest thou yet, Gazellus, to his foil:
Which we referred to justice of his Christ,
And to his power, which here appears as full
As rays of Cynthia to the clearest sight?   30

GAZELLUS
'Tis but the fortune of the wars my lord,
Whose power is often proved a miracle.

ORCANES
Yet in my thoughts shall Christ be honoured,
Not doing Mahomet an injury,
Whose power had share in this our victory: 35
And since this miscreant hath disgraced his faith,
And died a traitor both to heaven and earth,
We will both watch and ward shall keep his trunk
Amidst these plains, for fowls to prey upon.
Go Uribassa, give it straight in charge.   40

URIBASSA
I will my lord.   *Exit* URIBASSA

ORCANES
And now Gazellus, let us haste and meet
Our army and our brother of Jerusalem,
Of Soria, Trebizon, and Amasia,
And happily with full Natolian bowls   45
Of Greekish wine now let us celebrate
Our happy conquest and his angry fate.   *Exeunt*

27 *foil* defeat
29 *his* Christ's
30 *rays of Cynthia* moonlight
32 *proved* asserted to be
36 *miscreant* vile wretch
38 *watch and ward* guard, originally by night and day
40 *give . . . charge* command it immediately
43 *Our army* i.e., the main body of our army
47 *angry* grievous

22 *Flora.* The Roman goddess of springtime and flowers.
25 *Orcus.* Hades. Marlowe here fuses Moslem, Christian, and Greek notions of hell.
44 *Amasia.* A district of Anatolia in northern Asia Minor.

Act II, Scene iv

The arras is drawn, and ZENOCRATE *lies in her bed of state,*
TAMBURLAINE *sitting by her; three* PHYSICIANS *about her bed,*
tempering potions; THERIDAMAS, TECHELLES, USUMCASANE, *and*
the three sons [CALYPHAS, AMYRAS, CELEBINUS]

TAMBURLAINE
    Black is the beauty of the brightest day,
    The golden ball of heaven's eternal fire,
    That danced with glory on the silver waves:
    Now wants the fuel that inflamed his beams
    And all with faintness and for foul disgrace,   5
    He binds his temples with a frowning cloud,
    Ready to darken earth with endless night:
    Zenocrate that gave him light and life,
    Whose eyes shot fire from their ivory bowers,
    And tempered every soul with lively heat,   10
    Now by the malice of the angry skies,
    Whose jealousy admits no second mate,
    Draws in the comfort of her latest breath
    All dazzled with the hellish mists of death.
    Now walk the angels on the walls of heaven,   15
    As sentinels to warn th'immortal souls,
    To entertain divine Zenocrate.
    Apollo, Cynthia, and the ceaseless lamps
    That gently looked upon this loathsome earth,
    Shine downwards now no more, but deck the heavens   20
    To entertain divine Zenocrate.
    The crystal springs whose taste illuminates
    Refined eyes with an eternal sight,
    Like tried silver runs through Paradise
    To entertain divine Zenocrate.   25
    The cherubins and holy seraphins
    That sing and play before the King of Kings,
    Use all their voices and their instruments
    To entertain divine Zenocrate.
    And in this sweet and curious harmony,   30
    The god that tunes this music to our souls:

9 *bowers* i.e., the places where they were set
18 *Apollo, Cynthia* the sun, the moon
23 *Refined* given clearer sight
24 *tried* purified
30 *curious* exquisite

Holds out his hand in highest majesty
To entertain divine Zenocrate.
Then let some holy trance convey my thoughts,
Up to the palace of th'empyreal heaven: 35
That this my life may be as short to me
As are the days of sweet Zenocrate:
Physicians, will no physic do her good?

PHYSICIAN
My lord, your majesty shall soon perceive:
And if she pass this fit, the worst is past.   40

TAMBURLAINE
Tell me, how fares my fair Zenocrate?

ZENOCRATE
I fare my lord, as other empresses,
That when this frail and transitory flesh
Hath sucked the measure of that vital air
That feeds the body with his dated health,   45
Wanes with enforced and necessary change.

TAMBURLAINE
May never such a change transform my love
In whose sweet being I repose my life,
Whose heavenly presence beautified with health,
Gives light to Phoebus and the fixed stars,   50
Whose absence makes the sun and moon as dark
As when opposed in one diameter
Their spheres are mounted on the serpent's head,
Or else descended to his winding train:
Live still my love and so conserve my life,   55
Or dying, be the author of my death.

ZENOCRATE
Live still my lord, O let my sovereign live,
And sooner let the fiery element

35 *th'empyreal heaven* see note to Part One, II, vii, 15
45 *dated* having its preordained end
50 *Phoebus* the sun
51 *makes* O3–4 (make O1)   56 *author* O4 (anchor O1)

---

52 *opposed ... diameter*. i.e., when the earth is directly between the sun
   and the moon, or when the moon is directly between the sun and the
   earth.
53–4 *Their spheres ... train*. The 'serpent' is the constellation Draco (the
   Dragon). The moon's path intersects the ecliptic (thus causing an
   eclipse) at two points, the Dragon's head and tail (train).
58 *the fiery element*. The sphere of fire, separating the earth from the
   planetary bodies.

Dissolve, and make your kingdom in the sky,
Than this base earth should shroud your majesty: 60
For should I but suspect your death by mine,
The comfort of my future happiness
And hope to meet your highness in the heavens,
Turned to despair, would break my wretched breast,
And fury would confound my present rest.   65
But let me die my love, yet let me die,
With love and patience let your true love die:
Your grief and fury hurts my second life,
Yet let me kiss my lord before I die,
And let me die with kissing of my lord.   70
But since my life is lengthened yet a while,
Let me take leave of these my loving sons,
And of my lords whose true nobility
Have merited my latest memory:
Sweet sons farewell, in death resemble me,   75
And in your lives your father's excellency.
Some music, and my fit will cease my lord.

                                      They call music

TAMBURLAINE

Proud fury and intolerable fit,
That dares torment the body of my love,
And scourge the Scourge of the immortal God!   80
Now are those spheres where Cupid used to sit,
Wounding the world with wonder and with love,
Sadly supplied with pale and ghastly death:
Whose darts do pierce the centre of my soul.
Her sacred beauty hath enchanted heaven,   85
And had she lived before the siege of Troy,
Helen, whose beauty summoned Greece to arms,
And drew a thousand ships to Tenedos,
Had not been named in Homer's Iliads:
Her name had been in every line he wrote: 90
Or had those wanton poets, for whose birth
Old Rome was proud, but gazed a while on her,
Nor Lesbia, nor Corinna had been named,

68 *my second life* my life after death
77 *fit* a mortal crisis
81 *those spheres* her eyes   90 *Her* Zenocrate's

---

88 *Tenedos.* A small island off the Troad.
93 *Lesbia . . . Corinna.* Women celebrated in the love poetry of Catullus
and Ovid.

Zenocrate had been the argument
Of every epigram or elegy.   95
> *The music sounds, and she dies*

What, is she dead? Techelles, draw thy sword,
And wound the earth, that it may cleave in twain,
And we descend into th'infernal vaults,
To hale the Fatal Sisters by the hair,
And throw them in the triple moat of hell,   100
For taking hence my fair Zenocrate.
Casane and Theridamas, to arms!
Raise cavalieros higher than the clouds,
And with the cannon break the frame of heaven,
Batter the shining palace of the sun,   105
And shiver all the starry firmament:
For amorous Jove hath snatched my love from hence,
Meaning to make her stately queen of heaven.
What god soever holds thee in his arms,
Giving thee nectar and ambrosia,   110
Behold me here, divine Zenocrate,
Raving, impatient, desperate and mad,
Breaking my steeled lance, with which I burst
The rusty beams of Janus' temple doors,
Letting out death and tyrannizing war,   115
To march with me under this bloody flag,
And if thou pitiest Tamburlaine the Great,
Come down from heaven and live with me again!

THERIDAMAS

Ah good my lord be patient, she is dead,
And all this raging cannot make her live.   120
If words might serve, our voice hath rent the air,
If tears, our eyes have watered all the earth:
If grief, our murdered hearts have strained forth blood.
Nothing prevails, for she is dead my lord.

TAMBURLAINE

For she is dead? Thy words do pierce my soul: 125
Ah sweet Theridamas, say no more,
Though she be dead, yet let me think she lives,

94 *argument* subject, theme
103 *cavalieros* mounds on which cannon were placed
123 *murdered* ed. (murthered O1)

99 *Fatal Sisters.* See note to Part One, I, ii, 174 above.
114 *Janus' temple doors.* The doors of the temple of Janus in Rome were
    open in time of war, closed in time of peace.

And feed my mind that dies for want of her:
Where'er her soul be, thou shalt stay with me
Embalmed with cassia, ambergris and myrrh,   130
Not lapped in lead but in a sheet of gold,
And till I die thou shalt not be interred.
Then in as rich a tomb as Mausolus',
We both shall rest and have one epitaph
Writ in as many several languages,   135
As I have conquered kingdoms with my sword.
This cursed town will I consume with fire,
Because this place bereft me of my love:
The houses burnt, will look as if they mourned
And here will I set up her statue,   140
And march about it with my mourning camp,
Drooping and pining for Zenocrate.

                              The arras is drawn [*Exeunt*]

Act III, Scene i

Enter the KINGS OF TREBIZON *and* SORIA, *one bringing a sword,
and another a sceptre. Next* NATOLIA *and* JERUSALEM *with the
mperial crown. After,* CALLAPINE, *and after him* [ALMEDA *and*]
other Lords. ORCANES *and* JERUSALEM *crown* [CALLAPINE] *and the
other*[s] *give him the sceptre*

ORCANES
Callapinus Cyricelibes, otherwise Cybelius, son and suc-
cessive heir to the late mighty emperor Bajazeth, by the aid
of God and his friend Mahomet, Emperor of Natolia, Jerusalem, Trebizon, Soria, Amasia, Thracia, Illyria, Carmonia,
and all the hundred and thirty kingdoms late contributory to   5
his mighty father. Long live Callapinus, Emperor of Turkey!
CA LLAPINE
Thrice worthy kings of Natolia, and the rest,
I will requite your royal gratitudes
With all the benefits my empire yields:

130 *cassia* a fragrant shrub
131 *lapped in lead* placed in a leaden coffin
140 *statue* O3–4 (stature O1)
      s.d. [ALMEDA *and*] ed. (O1 omits) [CALLAPINE] ed. (him O1)

---

133 *Mausolus.* King of Caria, whose widow (also his sister) built for him
     a costly monument, called Mausoleum, at Halicarnassus.
  4 *Carmonia.* Carmania, south-east of Natolia and north of Syria.

And were the sinews of th'imperial seat   10
So knit and strengthened, as when Bajazeth,
My royal lord and father, filled the throne,
Whose cursed fate hath so dismembered it,
Then should you see this thief of Scythia,
This proud usurping King of Persia,   15
Do us such honour and supremacy,
Bearing the vengeance of our father's wrongs,
As all the world should blot our dignities
Out of the book of base-born infamies.
And now I doubt not but your royal cares   20
Hath so provided for this cursed foe,
That since the heir of mighty Bajazeth
(An emperor so honoured for his virtues)
Revives the spirit of true Turkish hearts,
In grievous memory of his father's shame,   25
We shall not need to nourish any doubt,
But that proud Fortune, who hath followed long
The martial sword of mighty Tamburlaine,
Will not retain her old inconstancy,
And raise our honours to as high a pitch   30
In this our strong and fortunate encounter.
For so hath heaven provided my escape,
From all the cruelty my soul sustained,
By this my friendly keeper's happy means,
That Jove, surcharged with pity of our wrongs,   35
Will pour it down in showers on our heads:
Scourging the pride of cursed Tamburlaine.

ORCANES
I have a hundred thousand men in arms,
Some, that in conquest of the perjured Christians,
Being a handful to a mighty host,   40
Think them in number yet sufficient,
To drink the river Nile or Euphrates,
And for their power, enow to win the world.

KING OF JERUSALEM
And I as many from Jerusalem,
Judea, Gaza, and Scalonians' bounds,   45
That on Mount Sinai with their ensigns spread,

18 *dignities* noble names
29 *retain* return to
43 *enow* enough
45 *Scalonians* the men of Scalonia (Ascalon)
46 *ensigns* banners

Look like the parti-coloured clouds of heaven,
That show fair weather to the neighbour morn.
KING OF TREBIZON
And I as many bring from Trebizon,
Chio, Famastro, and Amasia,   50
All bordering on the Mare Major sea:
Riso, Sancina, and the bordering towns
That touch the end of famous Euphrates,
Whose courages are kindled with the flames,
The cursed Scythian sets on all their towns,   55
And vow to burn the villain's cruel heart.
KING OF SORIA
From Soria with seventy thousand strong,
Ta'en from Aleppo, Soldino, Tripoli,
And so unto my city of Damascus
I march to meet and aid my neighbour kings,   60
All which will join against this Tamburlaine,
And bring him captive to your highness' feet.
ORCANES
Our battle then in martial manner pitched,
According to our ancient use, shall bear
The figure of the semi-circled moon: 65
Whose horns shall sprinkle through the tainted air,
The poisoned brains of this proud Scythian.
CALLAPINE
Well then my noble lords, for this my friend,
That freed me from the bondage of my foe:
I think it requisite and honourable,   70
To keep my promise, and to make him king,
That is a gentleman, I know, at least.
ALMEDA
That's no matter sir, for being a king, for Tamburlaine came
up of nothing.
KING OF JERUSALEM
Your majesty may choose some 'pointed time,   75
Performing all your promise to the full:
'Tis naught for your majesty to give a kingdom.
CALLAPINE
Then will I shortly keep my promise Almeda.
ALMEDA
Why, I thank your majesty.   *Exeunt*

64 *use* custom

---

51 *Mare Major sea.* The Black Sea.

Act III, Scene ii

[Enter] TAMBURLAINE *with* USUMCASANE, *and his three sons*
[CALYPHAS, AMYRAS, *and* CELEBINUS]; *four [Attendants] bearing
the hearse of* ZENOCRATE, *and the drums sounding a doleful march;
the town burning*

TAMBURLAINE

So, burn the turrets of this cursed town,
Flame to the highest region of the air:
And kindle heaps of exhalations,
That being fiery meteors, may presage,
Death and destruction to th'inhabitants.   5
Over my zenith hang a blazing star,
That may endure till heaven be dissolved,
Fed with the fresh supply of earthly dregs,
Threatening a death and famine to this land,
Flying dragons, lightning, fearful thunderclaps,   10
Singe these fair plains, and make them seem as black
As is the island where the Furies mask,
Compassed with Lethe, Styx, and Phlegethon,
Because my dear Zenocrate is dead.

CALYPHAS

This pillar placed in memory of her,   15
Where in Arabian, Hebrew, Greek, is writ,
'This town being burnt by Tamburlaine the Great,
Forbids the world to build it up again.'

AMYRAS

And here this mournful streamer shall be placed
Wrought with the Persian and Egyptian arms   20
To signify she was a princess born,
And wife unto the monarch of the East.

6 *zenith* the point directly above him
19 *streamer* pennon
20 *Wrought* embroidered

---

2 *highest . . . air.* The uppermost limit of the atmosphere, next to the
sphere of the moon.
3–5 *kindle . . . inhabitants.* May the rising flames create meteors, traditionally portents of disaster.
12 *island . . . mask.* The underworld is thought of as an island, presumably
because it is ringed with rivers. The Furies hide (mask) there until
called into the upper world.
13 *Lethe . . . Phlegethon.* Rivers of the underworld.

CELEBINUS

    And here this table as a register
    Of all her virtues and perfections.

TAMBURLAINE

    And here the picture of Zenocrate,   25
    To show her beauty, which the world admired,
    Sweet picture of divine Zenocrate,
    That hanging here, will draw the gods from heaven:
    And cause the stars fixed in the southern arc,
    Whose lovely faces never any viewed,   30
    That have not passed the centre's latitude,
    As pilgrims travel to our hemisphere,
    Only to gaze upon Zenocrate.
    Thou shalt not beautify Larissa plains,
    But keep within the circle of mine arms.   35
    At every town and castle I besiege,
    Thou shalt be set upon my royal tent.
    And when I meet an army in the field,
    Those looks will shed such influence in my camp,
    As if Bellona, goddess of the war,   40
    Threw naked swords and sulphur balls of fire,
    Upon the heads of all our enemies.
    And now my lords, advance your spears again,
    Sorrow no more my sweet Casane now:
    Boys, leave to mourn, this town shall ever mourn,   45
    Being burnt to cinders for your mother's death.

CALYPHAS

    If I had wept a sea of tears for her,
    It would not ease the sorrow I sustain.

AMYRAS

    As is that town, so is my heart consumed,
    With grief and sorrow for my mother's death.   50

CELEBINUS

    My mother's death hath mortified my mind,
    And sorrow stops the passage of my speech.

TAMBURLAINE

    But now my boys, leave off, and list to me,
    That mean to teach you rudiments of war:

23 *table* tablet
29 *arc* hemisphere
31 *centre's latitude* equator
41 *sulphur . . . fire* primitive incendiary bombs

---

40 *Bellona.* The Roman goddess of war.

I'll have you learn to sleep upon the ground,   55
March in your armour thorough watery fens,
Sustain the scorching heat and freezing cold,
Hunger and thirst, right adjuncts of the war.
And after this, to scale a castle wall,
Besiege a fort, to undermine a town,   60
And make whole cities caper in the air.
Then next, the way to fortify your men,
In champion grounds, what figure serves you best,
For which the quinque-angle form is meet,
Because the corners there may fall more flat: 65
Whereas the fort may fittest be assailed,
And sharpest where th'assault is desperate.
The ditches must be deep, the counterscarps
Narrow and steep, the walls made high and broad,
The bulwarks and the rampires large and strong,   70
With cavalieros and thick counterforts,
And room within to lodge six thousand men.
It must have privy ditches, countermines,
And secret issuings to defend the ditch.
It must have high argins and covered ways   75
To keep the bulwark fronts from battery,
And parapets to hide the musketeers:
Casemates to place the great artillery,
And store of ordnance that from every flank
May scour the outward curtains of the fort,   80

56 *thorough* O2–4 (throwe O1)   63 *champion* level and open
63 *figure* shape of fort   64 *which* ed. (with O1)
64 *quinque-angle* pentagonal (Tamburlaine is thinking of an irregular
    pentagon)
64 *meet* suitable   65 *fall more flat* form wider angles
66 *Whereas* where
67 *desperate* dangerous to undertake
68 *counterscarps* the outer walls of the ditch surrounding a fort
70 *bulwarks* projecting earthworks built round the angles of a fort
70 *rampires* ramparts supporting the walls from within
71 *cavalieros* mounds for heavy guns   75 *argins* earthworks
75 *covered ways* protected passages between earthworks and
    counterscarps
78 *Casemates* chambers within the ramparts of a fort
80 *curtains* walls connecting the towers

62–90 A close paraphrase of Paul Ive's *Practice of Fortification* (1589). See
    Paul Kocher, 'Marlowe's Art of War', *Studies in Philology*, xxxix (1942),
    207–25.

Dismount the cannon of the adverse part,
Murder the foe and save the walls from breach.
When this is learned for service on the land,
By plain and easy demonstration,
I'll teach you how to make the water mount,   85
That you may dry-foot march through lakes and pools,
Deep rivers, havens, creeks and little seas,
And make a fortress in the raging waves,
Fenced with the concave of a monstrous rock,
Invincible by nature of the place.   90
When this is done, then are ye soldiers,
And worthy sons of Tamburlaine the Great.

CALYPHAS
My lord, this is but dangerous to be done,
We may be slain or wounded ere we learn.

TAMBURLAINE
Villain, art thou the son of Tamburlaine,   95
And fear'st to die, or with a curtle-axe
To hew thy flesh and make a gaping wound?
Hast thou beheld a peal of ordnance strike
A ring of pikes, mingled with shot and horse,
Whose shattered limbs, being tossed as high as heaven,   100
Hang in the air as thick as sunny motes,
And canst thou, coward, stand in fear of death?
Hast thou not seen my horsemen charge the foe,
Shot through the arms, cut overthwart the hands,
Dyeing their lances with their streaming blood,   105
And yet at night carouse within my tent
Filling their empty veins with airy wine,
That being concocted, turns to crimson blood,
And wilt thou shun the field for fear of wounds?
View me thy father that hath conquered kings,   110
And with his host marched round about the earth,

81 *adverse part* adversary
82 *Murder* ed. (murther O1)
82 *the walls* ed. (their walles O1)
98 *peal of ordnance* discharge of cannon
99 *A ring ... horse* a ring of pike-men closely flanked by infantry
   and cavalry
101 *sunny motes* particles of dust in the sunlight
111 *marched* O3–4 (martch O1)

107–8 *Filling ... blood.* Loss of blood was thought to create a vacuum and
   wine, when digested (concocted), to turn to blood.

Quite void of scars, and clear from any wound,
That by the wars lost not a dram of blood,
And see him lance his flesh to teach you all.

He cuts his arm   115

A wound is nothing be it ne'er so deep,
Blood is the god of war's rich livery.
Now look I like a soldier, and this wound
As great a grace and majesty to me,
As if a chair of gold enamelled,
Enchased with diamonds, sapphires, rubies   120
And fairest pearl of wealthy India
Were mounted here under a canopy:
And I sat down clothed with the massy robe,
That late adorned the Afric potentate,
Whom I brought bound unto Damascus' walls.   125
Come boys and with your fingers search my wound,
And in my blood wash all your hands at once,
While I sit smiling to behold the sight.
Now my boys, what think you of a wound?

CALYPHAS
I know not what I should think of it. Methinks 'tis a pitiful   130
sight.

CELEBINUS
'Tis nothing: give me a wound father.

AMYRAS
And me another my lord.

TAMBURLAINE
Come sirrah, give me your arm.

CELEBINUS
Here father, cut it bravely as you did your own.   135

TAMBURLAINE
It shall suffice thou dar'st abide a wound.
My boy, thou shalt not lose a drop of blood,
Before we meet the army of the Turk.
But then run desperate through the thickest throngs,
Dreadless of blow, of bloody wounds and death: 140
And let the burning of Larissa walls,
My speech of war, and this my wound you see
Teach you my boys to bear courageous minds,
Fit for the followers of great Tamburlaine.
Usumcasane now come let us march   145

120 *Enchased* adorned
124 *Afric potentate* i.e., Bajazeth, so called from his African conquests
135 *bravely* well

Towards Techelles and Theridamas,
That we have sent before to fire the towns,
The towers and cities of these hateful Turks,
And hunt that coward, faintheart, runaway,
With that accursed traitor Almeda,   150
Till fire and sword have found them at a bay.

USUMCASANE
I long to pierce his bowels with my sword,
That hath betrayed my gracious sovereign,
That cursed and damned traitor Almeda.

ΤΑMBURLAINE
Then let us see if coward Callapine   155
Dare levy arms against our puissance,
That we may tread upon his captive neck,
And treble all his father's slaveries.   *Exeunt*

Act III, Scene iii

[*Enter*] TECHELLES, THERIDAMAS, *and their train* [*, Soldiers and
Pioners*]

THERIDAMAS
Thus have we marched northward from Tamburlaine,
Unto the frontier point of Soria:
And this is Balsera, their chiefest hold,
Wherein is all the treasure of the land.

TECHELLES
Then let us bring our light artillery,   5
Minions, falc'nets, and sakers, to the trench,
Filling the ditches with the walls' wide breach,
And enter in, to seize upon the gold:
How say ye soldiers, shall we not?

SOLDIERS
Yes, my lord, yes, come let's about it.   10

THERIDAMAS
But stay a while, summon a parle, drum,
It may be they will yield it quietly,
Knowing two kings, the friends to Tamburlaine,
Stand at the walls, with such a mighty power.

---

151 *at a bay* at bay   3 *hold* stronghold
6 *Minions . . . sakers* small pieces of ordnance

---

3 *Balsera.* Probably Passera, a town near the Natolian frontier indicated
on the maps of Ortelius.

Summon the battle. [*Enter*] CAPTAIN *with his wife* [OLYMPIA]
                              and SON [*above*]

CAPTAIN
   What require you my masters?   15
THERIDAMAS
   Captain, that thou yield up thy hold to us.
CAPTAIN
   To you? Why, do you think me weary of it?
TECHELLES
   Nay Captain, thou art weary of thy life,
   If thou withstand the friends of Tamburlaine.
THERIDAMAS
   These pioners of Argier in Africa,   20
   Even in the cannon's face shall raise a hill
   Of earth and faggots higher than thy fort,
   And over thy argins and covered ways
   Shall play upon the bulwarks of thy hold
   Volleys of ordnance till the breach be made,   25
   That with his ruin fills up all the trench.
   And when we enter in, not heaven itself
   Shall ransom thee, thy wife and family.
TECHELLES
   Captain, these Moors shall cut the leaden pipes,
   That bring fresh water to thy men and thee,   30
   And lie in trench before thy castle walls:
   That no supply of victual shall come in,
   Nor any issue forth, but they shall die:
   And therefore Captain, yield it quietly.
CAPTAIN
   Were you that are the friends of Tamburlaine   35
   Brothers to holy Mahomet himself,
   I would not yield it: therefore do your worst.
   Raise mounts, batter, intrench, and undermine,
   Cut off the water, all convoys that can,
   Yet I am resolute, and so farewell.   [*Exeunt above*] 40
THERIDAMAS
   Pioners away, and where I stuck the stake,
   Intrench with those dimensions I prescribed:
   Cast up the earth towards the castle wall,

14 s.d. [*above*] ed. (O1 omits)
26 *trench* defensive ditch around the outer walls
38 *intrench* surround with trenches
39 *convoys* supplies under escort   40 s.d. ed. (O1 omits)

Which till it may defend you, labour low:
And few or none may perish by their shot.   45

PIONERS

We will my lord.   *Exeunt* [PIONERS]

TECHELLES

A hundred horse shall scout about the plains
To spy what force comes to relieve the hold.
Both we, Theridamas, will intrench our men,
And with the Jacob's staff measure the height   50
And distance of the castle from the trench,
That we may know if our artillery
Will carry full point blank into their walls.

THERIDAMAS

Then see the bringing of our ordinance
Along the trench into the battery,   55
Where we will have gabions of six foot broad,
To save our cannoneers from musket shot,
Betwixt which, shall our ordnance thunder forth,
And with the breach's fall, smoke, fire, and dust,
The crack, the echo and the soldier's cry   60
Make deaf the air and dim the crystal sky.

TECHELLES

Trumpets and drums, alarum presently!
And, soldiers, play the men, the hold is yours.   [*Exeunt*]

Act III, Scene iv

Enter the CAPTAIN *with his wife* [OLYMPIA] *and* SON

OLYMPIA

Come good my lord, and let us haste from hence
Along the cave that leads beyond the foe,
No hope is left to save this conquered hold.

46 s.d. [PIONERS] ed. (O1 omits)
50 *Jacob's staff* an instrument used for measuring heights and distances
56 *gabions* ed. (Gabious O1) great baskets filled with earth, used in defence and to steady cannons
62 *alarum* call to arms   62 *presently* at once, immediately
63 *hold* O2–3 (holds O1)   63 s.d. ed. (O1 omits)
          s.d. [OLYMPIA] ed. (O1 omits)
 2 *cave* underground passage

54 *ordinance* Marlowe's usual spelling of 'ordnance', here retained for the sake of the metre.

CAPTAIN

A deadly bullet gliding through my side,
Lies heavy on my heart, I cannot live.   5
I feel my liver pierced and all my veins,
That there begin and nourish every part,
Mangled and torn, and all my entrails bathed
In blood that straineth from their orifex.
Farewell sweet wife! Sweet son farewell! I die.   [*Dies*]   10

OLYMPIA

Death, whither art thou gone that both we live?
Come back again, sweet Death, and strike us both:
One minute end our days, and one sepulcher
Contain our bodies: Death, why com'st thou not?
Well, this must be the messenger for thee.   15
Now ugly Death stretch out thy sable wings,
And carry both our souls, where his remains.
Tell me sweet boy, art thou content to die?
These barbarous Scythians full of cruelty,
And Moors, in whom was never pity found,   20
Will hew us piecemeal, put us to the wheel,
Or else invent some torture worse than that,
Therefore die by thy living mother's hand,
Who gently now will lance thy ivory throat,
And quickly rid thee both of pain and life.   25

SON

Mother dispatch me, or I'll kill myself,
For think ye I can live and see him dead?
Give me your knife, good mother, or strike home:
The Scythians shall not tyrannize on me.
Sweet mother strike, that I may meet my father.   30
                                        She stabs him

OLYMPIA

Ah sacred Mahomet, if this be sin,
Intreat a pardon of the God of heaven,
And purge my soul before it come to thee.

Enter THERIDAMAS, TECHELLES *and all their train*

THERIDAMAS

How now madam, what are you doing?

OLYMPIA

Killing myself, as I have done my son,   35

9 *orifex* orifice, breach
10 s.d. ed. (O1 omits)
21 *the wheel* an instrument of torture

Whose body with his father's I have burnt,
Lest cruel Scythians should dismember him.

TECHELLES

'Twas bravely done, and like a soldier's wife.
Thou shalt with us to Tamburlaine the Great,
Who when he hears how resolute thou wert,   40
Will match thee with a viceroy or a king.

OLYMPIA

My lord deceased, was dearer unto me,
Than any viceroy, king or emperor,
And for his sake here will I end my days.

THERIDAMAS

But lady go with us to Tamburlaine,   45
And thou shalt see a man greater than Mahomet,
In whose high looks is much more majesty
Than from the concave superficies
Of Jove's vast palace the imperial orb,
Unto the shining bower where Cynthia sits,   50
Like lovely Thetis in a crystal robe:
That treadeth fortune underneath his feet,
And makes the mighty god of arms his slave:
On whom Death and the Fatal Sisters wait,
With naked swords and scarlet liveries: 55
Before whom, mounted on a lion's back,
Rhamnusia bears a helmet full of blood,
And strows the way with brains of slaughtered men
By whose proud side the Ugly Furies run,
Harkening when he shall bid them plague the world   60
Over whose zenith clothed in windy air,
And eagle's wings joined to her feathered breast,
Fame hovereth, sounding of her golden trump:
That to the adverse poles of that straight line,

48 *superficies* bounds
49 *orb* sphere
61 *zenith* crest; the highest point in his career
64–5 *adverse . . . heaven* the diameter of the sphere of heaven

---

47–51 'In Tamburlaine's looks there dwells more majesty than is to be
found throughout the heavens, from the hollow roof of Jove's palace
to the shining bower where the moon sits veiled in a crystal robe like
Thetis the ocean goddess' (Ellis-Fermor).
53 *god of arms.* Mars.
54 *Fatal Sisters.* The Fates.
57 *Rhamnusia.* Nemesis.

Which measureth the glorious frame of heaven,　　　　65
The name of mighty Tamburlaine is spread:
And him, fair lady, shall thy eyes behold.
Come.

OLYMPIA
Take pity of a lady's ruthful tears,
That humbly craves upon her knees to stay,　　　　70
And cast her body in the burning flame,
That feeds upon her son's and husband's flesh.

TECHELLES
Madam, sooner shall fire consume us both,
That scorch a face so beautiful as this,
In frame of which, nature hath showed more skill,　　　　75
Than when she gave eternal chaos form,
Drawing from it the shining lamps of heaven.

THERIDAMAS
Madam, I am so far in love with you,
That you must go with us, no remedy.

OLYMPIA
Then carry me I care not where you will,　　　　80
And let the end of this my fatal journey,
Be likewise end to my accursed life.

TECHELLES
No madam, but the beginning of your joy,
Come willingly therefore.

THERIDAMAS
Soldiers now let us meet the general,　　　　85
Who by this time.is at Natolia,
Ready to charge the army of the Turk.
The gold, the silver, and the pearl ye got,
Rifling this fort, divide in equal shares:
This lady shall have twice so much again,　　　　90
Out of the coffers of our treasury.　　　　　　　*Exeunt*

Act III, Scene v

[*Enter*] CALLAPINE, ORCANES, JERUSALEM, TREBIZON, SORIA,
　　ALMEDA, *with their train* [*and* MESSENGER]

MESSENGER
Renowned emperor, mighty Callapine,
God's great lieutenant over all the world:

67–8 lineation ed.
　75 *frame* forming, fashioning

Here at Aleppo with an host of men
Lies Tamburlaine, this King of Persia:
In number more than are the quivering leaves   5
Of Ida's forest, where your highness' hounds,
With open cry pursues the wounded stag:
Who means to girt Natolia's walls with siege,
Fire the town and overrun the land.

CALLAPINE
My royal army is as great as his,   10
That from the bounds of Phrygia to the sea
Which washeth Cyprus with his brinish waves,
Covers the hills, the valleys and the plains.
Viceroys and peers of Turkey, play the men,
Whet all your swords to mangle Tamburlaine,   15
His sons, his captains and his followers,
By Mahomet not one of them shall live.
The field wherein this battle shall be fought,
Forever term, the Persians' sepulchre,
In memory of this our victory.   20

ORCANES
Now, he that calls himself the Scourge of Jove,
The emperor of the world and earthly god,
Shall end the warlike progress he intends,
And travel headlong to the lake of hell:
Where legions of devils (knowing he must die   25
Here in Natolia, by your highness' hands)
All brandishing their brands of quenchless fire,
Stretching their monstrous paws, grin with their teeth,
And guard the gates to entertain his soul.

CALLAPINE
Tell me viceroys the number of your men,   30
And what our army royal is esteemed.

KING OF JERUSALEM
From Palestina and Jerusalem,
Of Hebrews, three score thousand fighting men
Are come since last we showed your majesty.

ORCANES
So from Arabia Desert, and the bounds   35
Of that sweet land, whose brave metropolis

---

6 *Ida's forest.* Either Mt Ida in Crete or Mt Ida near Troy.
8 *Natolia.* Asia Minor, but here apparently a city.
11 *Phrygia.* An inland district of Natolia.
36 *metropolis.* Babylon, whose walls were supposedly built by Semiramis.

Re-edified the fair Semiramis,
Came forty thousand warlike foot and horse,
Since last we numbered to your majesty.

KING OF TREBIZON
From Trebizon in Asia the Less,   40
Naturalized Turks and stout Bithynians
Came to my bands full fifty thousand more,
That fighting, knows not what retreat doth mean,
Nor ere return but with the victory,
Since last we numbered to your majesty.   45

KING OF SORIA
Of Sorians from Halla is repaired
And neighbour cities of your highness' land,
Ten thousand horse, and thirty thousand foot,
Since last we numbered to your majesty:
So that the royal army is esteemed   50
Six hundred thousand valiant fighting men.

CALLAPINE
Then welcome, Tamburlaine, unto thy death.
Come puissant viceroys, let us to the field,
The Persians' sepulchre, and sacrifice
Mountains of breathless men to Mahomet,   55
Who now with Jove opens the firmament,
To see the slaughter of our enemies.

[*Enter*] TAMBURLAINE *with his three sons* [CALYPHAS, AMYRAS,
and CELEBINUS], USUMCASANE, *with other*[*s*]

TAMBURLAINE
How now Casane? See a knot of kings,
Sitting as they were a-telling riddles.

USUMCASANE
My lord, your presence makes them pale and wan.   60
Poor souls they look as if their deaths were near.

TAMBURLAINE
Why so he is Casane, I am here,
But yet I'll save their lives and make them slaves.
Ye petty kings of Turkey I am come,

---

41 *stout* bold

---

40 *Asia the Less.* Asia Minor.
41 *Bithynians.* Bithynia was the north-western region of Asia Minor.
46 *Halla.* A town to the south-east of Aleppo.

As Hector did into the Grecian camp,   65
To overdare the pride of Graecia,
And set his warlike person to the view
Of fierce Achilles, rival of his fame.
I do you honour in the simile,
For if I should as Hector did Achilles   70
(The worthiest knight that ever brandished sword),
Challenge in combat any of you all,
I see how fearfully ye would refuse,
And fly my glove as from a scorpion.

ORCANES
Now thou art fearful of thy army's strength,   75
Thou wouldst with overmatch of person fight;
But shepherd's issue, base-born Tamburlaine,
Think of thy end, this sword shall lance thy throat.

TAMBURLAINE
Villain, the shepherd's issue, at whose birth
Heaven did afford a gracious aspect,   80
And joined those stars that shall be opposite,
Even till the dissolution of the world,
And never meant to make a conqueror,
So famous as the mighty Tamburlaine:
Shall so torment thee and that Callapine,   85
That like a roguish runaway, suborned
That villain there, that slave, that Turkish dog,
To false his service to his sovereign,
As ye shall curse the birth of Tamburlaine.

CALLAPINE
Rail not Scythian, I shall now revenge   90
My father's vile abuses and mine own.

KING OF JERUSALEM
By Mahomet, he shall be tied in chains,
Rowing with Christians in a brigandine,

74 *glove* throw down a challenge
76 *with ... fight* fight personally, out of confidence in your superior
    strength
80 *gracious aspect* favourable conjunction of the heavenly bodies
81-2 *And joined ... world* which conjunction will never again be seen
88 *false* betray
93 *brigandine* brigantine

65-8 *As Hector ... fame.* There is no such episode in the *Iliad*, but
     Marlowe could have found it in the post-Homeric Troy tales, such as
     Lydgate's *Troy Book.*

About the Grecian isles to rob and spoil:
And turn him to his ancient trade again.   95
Methinks the slave should make a lusty thief. 3

CALLAPINE
Nay, when the battle ends, all we will meet,
And sit in council to invent some pain,
That may most vex his body and his soul.

TAMBURLAINE
Sirrah, Callapine, I'll hang a clog about your neck for run-   100
ning away again, you shall not trouble me thus to come and
fetch you.
But as for you, viceroy, you shall have bits,
And harnessed like my horses, draw my coach:
And when ye stay, be lashed with whips of wire;   105
I'll have you learn to feed on provender
And in a stable lie upon the planks.

ORCANES
But Tamburlaine, first thou shalt kneel to us
And humbly crave a pardon for thy life.

KING OF TREBIZON
The common soldiers of our mighty host   110
Shall bring thee bound unto the general's tent.

KING OF SORIA
And all have jointly sworn thy cruel death,
Or bind thee in eternal torments' wrath.

TAMBURLAINE
Well sirs, diet yourselves, you know I shall have occasion
shortly to journey you.   115

CELEBINUS
See father, how Almeda the jailor looks upon us.

TAMBURLAINE
Villain, traitor, damned fugitive,
I'll make thee wish the earth had swallowed thee:
Seest thou not death within my wrathful looks?
Go villain, cast thee headlong from a rock,   120
Or rip thy bowels, and rend out thy heart,
T'appease my wrath, or else I'll torture thee,
Searing thy hateful flesh with burning irons,
And drops of scalding lead, while all thy joints
Be racked and beat asunder with the wheel,   125

96 *lusty* vigorous
100 *for* to prevent
114 *diet yourselves* feed yourself well
115 *journey* drive (as horses)

For if thou livest, not any element
Shall shroud thee from the wrath of Tamburlaine.

CALLAPINE

Well, in despite of thee he shall be king:
Come Almeda, receive this crown of me.
I here invest thee King of Ariadan,   130
Bordering on Mare Roso near to Mecca.

ORCANES

What! take it man.

ALMEDA

Good my lord, let me take it.

CALLAPINE

Dost thou ask him leave? Here, take it.

TAMBURLAINE

Go to sirrah, take your crown, and make up the half dozen.   135
So sirrah, now you are a king you must give arms.

ORCANES

So he shall, and wear thy head in his scutcheon.

TAMBURLAINE

No, let him hang a bunch of keys on his standard, to put him
in remembrance he was a jailor, that when I take him, I may
knock out his brains with them, and lock you in the stable,   140
when you shall come sweating from my chariot.

KING OF TREBIZON

Away, let us to the field, that the villain may be slain.

TAMBURLAINE

Sirrah, prepare whips, and bring my chariot to my tent: for
as soon as the battle is done, I'll ride in triumph through the
camp.   145

Enter THERIDAMAS, TECHELLES, *and their train*

How now ye petty kings, lo, here are bugs
Will make the hair stand upright on your heads,
And cast your crowns in slavery at their feet.
Welcome Theridamas and Techelles both,
See ye this rout, and know ye this same king?   150

THERIDAMAS

Ay, my lord, he was Callapine's keeper.

137 *scutcheon* heraldic shield
146 *bugs* bugbears

---

130 *Ariadan.* According to Ortelius, on the Red Sea coast of Arabia, south
of Mecca.
131 *Mare Roso.* The Red Sea.

TAMBURLAINE
　　Well, now you see he is a king, look to him Theridamas,
　　when we are fighting, lest he hide his crown as the foolish
　　King of Persia did.

KING OF SORIA
　　No, Tamburlaine, he shall not be put to that exigent, I　155
　　warrant thee.

TAMBURLAINE
　　You know not sir:
　　But now my followers and my loving friends,
　　Fight as you ever did, like conquerors,
　　The glory of this happy day is yours:　　　　　　　160
　　My stern aspect shall make fair victory,
　　Hovering betwixt our armies, light on me,
　　Loaden with laurel wreaths to crown us all.

TECHELLES
　　I smile to think, how when this field is fought,
　　And rich Natolia ours, our men shall sweat　　　　165
　　With carrying pearl and treasure on their backs.

TAMBURLAINE
　　You shall be princes all immediately:
　　Come fight ye Turks, or yield us victory.

ORCANES
　　No, we will meet thee slavish Tamburlaine.　　　*Exeunt*

Act IV, Scene i

Alarm. AMYRAS *and* CELEBINUS *issues from the tent where*
CALYPHAS *sits asleep*

AMYRAS
　　Now in their glories shine the golden crowns
　　Of these proud Turks, much like so many suns
　　That half dismay the majesty of heaven:
　　Now brother, follow we our father's sword,
　　That flies with fury swifter than our thoughts,　　　5
　　And cuts down armies with his conquering wings.

CELEBINUS
　　Call forth our lazy brother from the tent,
　　For if my father miss him in the field,
　　Wrath kindled in the furnace of his breast,
　　Will send a deadly lightning to his heart.　　　　10

163 *Loaden* laden
　1 s.p. ed. (O1 omits)　　　　*conquering* ed. (conquerings O1)

AMYRAS

    Brother ho! What, given so much to sleep
    You cannot leave it, when our enemies' drums
    And rattling cannons thunder in our ears
    Our proper ruin and our father's foil?

CALYPHAS

    Away ye fools, my father needs not me,   15
    Nor you, in faith, but that you will be thought
    More childish valourous than manly wise:
    If half our camp should sit and sleep with me,
    My father were enough to scare the foe:
    You do dishonour to his majesty,   20
    To think our helps will do him any good.

AMYRAS

    What, dar'st thou then be absent from the fight,
    Knowing my father hates thy cowardice,
    And oft hath warned thee to be still in field,
    When he himself amidst the thickest troops   25
    Beats down our foes to flesh our taintless swords?

CALYPHAS

    I know sir, what it is to kill a man,
    It works remorse of conscience in me,
    I take no pleasure to be murderous,
    Nor care for blood when wine will quench my thirst.   30

CELEBINUS

    O cowardly boy! Fie, for shame, come forth!
    Thou dost dishonour manhood and thy house.

CALYPHAS

    Go, go tall stripling, fight you for us both,
    And take my other toward brother here,
    For person like to prove a second Mars.   35
    'Twill please my mind as well to hear both you
    Have won a heap of honour in the field,
    And left your slender carcasses behind,
    As if I lay with you for company.

AMYRAS

    You will not go then?   40

CALYPHAS

    You say true.

14 *proper* own   14 *foil* defeat
26 *to flesh . . . swords* to fight our first battle
29 *murderous* ed. (murtherous O1)
33 *tall* brave
34 *toward* forward, promising

AMYRAS
Were all the lofty mounts of Zona Mundi,
That fill the midst of farthest Tartary,
Turned into pearl and proffered for my stay,
I would not bide the fury of my father: 45
When made a victor in these haughty arms,
He comes and finds his sons have had no shares
In all the honours he proposed for us.
CALYPHAS
Take you the honour, I will take my ease,
My wisdom shall excuse my cowardice: 50
I go into the field before I need?
    Alarm, and AMYRAS *and* CELEBINUS *run in*
The bullets fly at random where they list.
And should I go and kill a thousand men,
I were as soon rewarded with a shot,
And sooner far than he that never fights.   55
And should I go and do nor harm nor good,
I might have harm, which all the good I have
Joined with my father's crown would never cure.
I'll to cards. Perdicas!

     [Enter PERDICAS]

PERDICAS
     Here my lord.
CALYPHAS
Come, thou and I will go to cards to drive away the time.   60
PERDICAS
Content my lord, but what shall we play for?
CALYPHAS
Who shall kiss the fairest of the Turks' concubines first,
when my father hath conquered them.
PERDICAS
Agreed i'faith.
         They play
CALYPHAS
They say I am a coward, Perdicas, and I fear as little their   65
taratantaras, their swords or their cannons, as I do a naked
lady in a net of gold, and for fear I should be afraid, would
put it off and come to bed with me.

52 *list* like
59 s.d. ed. (O1 omits)   66 *taratantaras* bugle calls

42 *Zona Mundi.* A mountain range in Tartary.

PERDICAS

Such a fear, my lord, would never make ye retire.

CALYPHAS

I would my father would let me be put in the front of such a   70
battle once, to try my valour.   *Alarm*
What a coil they keep, I believe there will be some hurt done
anon amongst them.   [*Exeunt*]

Enter TAMBURLAINE, THERIDAMAS, TECHELLES, USUMCASANE,
AMYRAS, CELEBINUS, *leading the Turkish Kings* [*of* NATOLIA,
JERUSALEM, TREBIZON, *and* SORIA; *and* SOLDIERS]

TAMBURLAINE

See now ye slaves, my children stoops your pride
And leads your glories sheep-like to the sword.   75
Bring them my boys, and tell me if the wars
Be not a life that may illustrate gods,
And tickle not your spirits with desire
Still to be trained in arms and chivalry?

AMYRAS

Shall we let go these kings again my lord   80
To gather greater numbers 'gainst our power,
That they may say, it is not chance doth this,
But matchless strength and magnanimity?

TAMBURLAINE

No, no Amyras, tempt not fortune so,
Cherish thy valour still with fresh supplies: 85
And glut it not with stale and daunted foes.
But where's this coward, villain, not my son,
But traitor to my name and majesty?
                           He goes in and brings him out
Image of sloth, and picture of a slave,
The obloquy and scorn of my renown,   90
How may my heart, thus fired with mine eyes,
Wounded with shame and killed with discontent,
Shroud any thought may hold my striving hands
From martial justice on thy wretched soul?

THERIDAMAS

Yet pardon him I pray your majesty.   95

72 *coil* commotion
73 s.d. ed. (O1 omits)
74 *stoops* make stoop   77 *illustrate* adorn, shed lustre upon
93 *Shroud* shelter, harbour
93 *may* which may

TECHELLES, USUMCASANE
   Let all of us entreat your highness' pardon.
TAMBURLAINE
   Stand up, ye base unworthy soldiers,
   Know ye not yet the argument of arms?
AMYRAS
   Good my lord, let him be forgiven for once,
   And we will force him to the field hereafter.   100
TAMBURLAINE
   Stand up my boys, and I will teach ye arms,
   And what the jealousy of wars must do.
   O Samarcanda, where I breathed first,
   And joyed the fire of this martial flesh,
   Blush, blush fair city at thine honour's foil   105
   And shame of nature which Jaertis' stream,
   Embracing thee with deepest of his love,
   Can never wash from thy distained brows,
   Here Jove, receive his fainting soul again,
   A form not meet to give that subject essence,   110
   Whose matter is the flesh of Tamburlaine,
   Wherein an incorporeal spirit moves,
   Made of the mould whereof thyself consists,
   Which makes me valiant, proud, ambitious,
   Ready to levy power against thy throne,   115
   That I might move the turning spheres of heaven,
   For earth and all this airy region

  98 *argument of arms* necessity of military life
102 *jealousy* zeal
104 *joyed . . flesh* indulged the desires of this warlike frame
105 *foil* disgrace
106 *which* ed. (with O1)
108 *distained* stained, dishonoured

---

103 *Samarcanda.* Samarkand, Tamburlaine's birthplace.
106 *Jaertis' stream.* The river Jaxartes, which flows east from Tartary to the
    Caspian Sea.
109–13 *Here Jove ... consists.* Ellis-Fermor paraphrases: 'Here Jove
    receive again the soul of Calyphas, a spirit (i.e., "form" almost in the
    sense of "idea") not worthy to be the immortal part (essence) of that
    subject whose mortal part (matter) is derived from the flesh of Tam-
    burlaine—in whom moves an immortal spirit of the same mould as
    thine own,' etc. She observes that 'form', 'subject', 'essence', and
    'matter' are used in strict accordance with the tradition of sixteenth-
    century Aristotelian logic, and that the whole passage throws an inter-
    esting light on Marlowe's conception of the dignity of man.

Cannot contain the state of Tamburlaine.

[Stabs CALYPHAS]

By Mahomet, thy mighty friend I swear,
In sending to my issue such a soul,   120
Created of the massy dregs of earth,
The scum and tartar of the elements,
Wherein was neither courage, strength, or wit,
But folly, sloth, and damned idleness:
Thou hast procured a greater enemy,   125
Than he that darted mountains at thy head,
Shaken the burthen mighty Atlas bears:
Whereat thou trembling hidd'st thee in the air,
Clothed with a pitchy cloud for being seen.
And now ye cankered curs of Asia,   130
That will not see the strength of Tamburlaine,
Although it shine as brightly as the sun:
Now you shall feel the strength of Tamburlaine,
And by the state of his supremacy,
Approve the difference 'twixt himself and you.   135

ORCANES

Thou showest the difference 'twixt ourselves and thee
In this thy barbarous damned tyranny.

KING OF JERUSALEM

Thy victories are grown so violent,
That shortly heaven, filled with the meteors
Of blood and fire thy tyrannies have made,   140
Will pour down blood and fire on thy head:
Whose scalding drops will pierce thy seething brains,
And with our bloods, revenge our bloods on thee.

TAMBURLAINE

Villains, these terrors and these tyrannies
(If tyrannies war's justice ye repute)   145
I execute, enjoined me from above:
To scourge the pride of such as heaven abhors,
Nor am I made arch-monarch of the world,

118 s.d. ed. (O1 omits)
122 *tartar* dregs (as of a wine cask)
129 *for being seen* to avoid being seen
135 *Approve* find out by experience
145 *repute* regard as

---

126 *he . . . head.* The Titans who warred against Jove.
127 *Atlas.* The Titan who was condemned to bear the heavens on his head
and hands.

Crowned and invested by the hand of Jove,
For deeds of bounty or nobility: 150
But since I exercise a greater name,
The Scourge of God and terror of the world,
I must apply myself to fit those terms,
In war, in blood, in death, in cruelty,
And plague such peasants as resist in me   155
The power of heaven's eternal majesty.
Theridamas, Techelles, and Casane,
Ransack the tents and the pavilions
Of these proud Turks, and take their concubines,
Making them bury this effeminate brat,   160
For not a common soldier shall defile
His manly fingers with so faint a boy.
Then bring those Turkish harlots to my tent,
And I'll dispose them as it likes me best,
Meanwhile take him in.
SOLDIERS   We will my lord.   165
        [*Exeunt* SOLDIERS *with the body of* CALYPHAS]
KING OF JERUSALEM
O damned monster, nay a fiend of hell,
Whose cruelties are not so harsh as thine,
Nor yet imposed with such a bitter hate!
ORCANES
Revenge it Rhadamanth and Aeacus,
And let your hates extended in his pains   170
Expel the hate wherewith he pains our souls!
KING OF TREBIZON
May never day give virtue to his eyes,
Whose sight composed of fury and of fire
Doth send such stern affections to his heart!
KING OF SORIA
May never spirit, vein or artier feed   175
The cursed substance of that cruel heart,

155 *resist in* ed. (resisting O1)
162 *faint* faint-hearted
164 *likes* pleases
165 s.d. ed. (O1 omits)
172 *virtue* power
174 *affections* emotions
175 *artier* artery

169 *Rhadamanth and Aeacus.* With Minos, the judges of the Greek under-
    world.

But, wanting moisture and remorseful blood,
Dry up with anger, and consume with heat!
TAMBURLAINE
Well, bark ye dogs. I'll bridle all your tongues
And bind them close with bits of burnished steel,   180
Down to the channels of your hateful throats,
And with the pains my rigour shall inflict,
I'll make ye roar, that earth may echo forth
The far resounding torments ye sustain,
As when an herd of lusty Cimbrian bulls,   185
Run mourning round about the females' miss,
And stung with fury of their following,
Fill all the air with troublous bellowing:
I will with engines, never exercised,
Conquer, sack, and utterly consume   190
Your cities and your golden palaces,
And with the flames that beat against the clouds
Incense the heavens, and make the stars to melt,
As if they were the tears of Mahomet
For hot consumption of his country's pride: 195
And till by vision, or by speech I hear
Immortal Jove say, cease my Tamburlaine,
I will persist a terror to the world,
Making the meteors, that like armed men
Are seen to march upon the towers of heaven,   200
Run tilting round about the firmament,
And break their burning lances in the air,
For honour of my wondrous victories.
Come bring them in to our pavilion.   *Exeunt*

Act IV, Scene ii

[Enter] OLYMPIA *alone*

[OLYMPIA]
Distressed Olympia, whose weeping eyes

177 *remorseful* compassionate
186 *females' miss* i.e., the loss of their mates
187 *their following* following them
193 *Incense* set on fire   201 *tilting* engaging in combat for sport
1 s.p. ed. (O1 omits)

185 *Cimbrian*. The Cimbri were a Celtic people who defeated several Roman armies in the second century B.C. Marlowe's association of the Cimbri with bulls apparently derives from Spenser's *Faerie Queene*, I, viii, 11.

Since thy arrival here beheld no sun,
But closed within the compass of a tent,
Hath stained thy cheeks, and made thee look like death,
Devise some means to rid thee of thy life,   5
Rather than yield to his detested suit,
Whose drift is only to dishonour thee.
And since this earth, dewed with thy brinish tears,
Affords no herbs, whose taste may poison thee,
Nor yet this air, beat often with thy sighs,   10
Contagious smells, and vapours to infect thee,
Nor thy close cave a sword to murder thee,
Let this invention be the instrument.

Enter THERIDAMAS

THERIDAMAS
Well met Olympia, I sought thee in thy tent
But when I saw the place obscure and dark,   15
Which with thy beauty thou wast wont to light,
Enraged, I ran about the fields for thee,
Supposing amorous Jove had sent his son,
The winged Hermes, to convey thee hence:
But now I find thee, and that fear is past.   20
Tell me Olympia, wilt thou grant my suit?
OLYMPIA
My lord and husband's death, with my sweet son's,
With whom I buried all affections,
Save grief and sorrow which torment my heart,
Forbids my mind to entertain a thought   25
That tends to love, but meditate on death,
A fitter subject for a pensive soul.
THERIDAMAS
Olympia, pity him, in whom thy looks
Have greater operation and more force
Than Cynthia's in the watery wilderness,   30
For with thy view my joys are at the full,
And ebb again as thou depart'st from me.
OLYMPIA
Ah pity me my lord, and draw your sword,

7 *drift* intention   12 *close* hidden
12 *murder* ed. (murther O1)
30 *Cynthia's . . . wilderness* i.e., the power of the moon to govern the
    tides

19 *Hermes.* Zeus's herald and messenger.

Making a passage for my troubled soul,
Which beats against this prison to get out,   35
And meet my husband and my loving son.

THERIDAMAS
Nothing, but still thy husband and thy son?
Leave this my love, and listen more to me,
Thou shalt be stately queen of fair Argier,
And clothed in costly cloth of massy gold,   40
Upon the marble turrets of thy court
Sit like to Venus in her chair of state,
Commanding all thy princely eye desires,
And I will cast off arms and sit with thee,
Spending my life in sweet discourse of love.   45

OLYMPIA
No such discourse is pleasant in mine ears,
Than that where every period ends with death,
And every line begins with death again:
I cannot love, to be an emperess.

THERIDAMAS
Nay lady, then if nothing will prevail,   50
I'll use some other means to make you yield,
Such is the sudden fury of my love,
I must and will be pleased, and you shall yield:
Come to the tent again.

OLYMPIA
Stay good my lord, and will you save my honour,   55
I'll give your grace a present of such price,
As all the world cannot afford the like.

THERIDAMAS
What is it?

OLYMPIA
An ointment which a cunning alchemist
Distilled from the purest balsamum,   60
And simplest extracts of all minerals,
In which the essential form of marble stone,
Tempered by science metaphysical,
And spells of magic from the mouths of spirits,
With which if you but 'noint your tender skin,   65
Nor pistol, sword, nor lance can pierce your flesh.

47 *period* sentence
61 *simplest extracts* in alchemy, the pure elements
62 *essential form* the fundamental quality of a spirit
63 *metaphysical* supernatural, the science that went beyond physical
   knowledge

THERIDAMAS
  Why madam, think ye to mock me thus palpably?
OLYMPIA
  To prove it, I will 'noint my naked throat,
  Which when you stab, look on your weapon's point,
  And you shall see't rebated with the blow.   70
THERIDAMAS
  Why gave you not your husband some of it,
  If you loved him, and it so precious?
OLYMPIA
  My purpose was, my lord, to spend it so,
  But was prevented by his sudden end,
  And for a present easy proof hereof,   75
  That I dissemble not, try it on me.
THERIDAMAS
  I will Olympia, and will keep it for
  The richest present of this eastern world.
                             She anoints her throat
OLYMPIA
  Now stab my lord, and mark your weapon's point
  That will be blunted if the blow be great.   80
THERIDAMAS
  Here then Olympia.
                       [He stabs her. She dies]
  What, have I slain her? Villain, stab thyself:
  Cut off this arm that murdered my love:
  In whom the learned rabbis of this age
  Might find as many wondrous miracles,   85
  As in the theoria of the world.
  Now hell is fairer than Elysium,
  A greater lamp than that bright eye of heaven,
  From whence the stars do borrow all their light,
  Wanders about the black circumference,   90
  And now the damned souls are free from pain,
  For every Fury gazeth on her looks:
  Infernal Dis is courting of my love,

70 *rebated* blunted
71–2 lineation ed. (O1 prints as prose)
81 s.d. ed. (O1 omits)
83 *murdered* ed. (murthered O1)
84 *rabbis* scholarly authorities
86 *theoria* observation, survey   87 *Elysium* ed. (Elisian O1)

93 *Dis.* Hades, Pluto, god of the underworld.

Inventing masks and stately shows for her,
Opening the doors of his rich treasury, 95
To entertain this queen of chastity,
Whose body shall be tombed with all the pomp
The treasure of my kingdom may afford.

Act IV, Scene iii

[Enter] TAMBURLAINE *drawn in his chariot by* TREBIZON *and* SORIA *with bits in their mouths, reins in his left hand, in his right hand a whip, with which he scourgeth them.* TECHELLES, THERIDAMAS, USUMCASANE, AMYRAS, CELEBINUS; [ORCANES, KING OF] NATOLIA, *and* JERUSALEM, *led by five or six common* SOLDIERS

TAMBURLAINE
Holla, ye pampered jades of Asia:
What, can ye draw but twenty miles a day,
And have so proud a chariot at your heels,
And such a coachman as great Tamburlaine?
But from Asphaltis, where I conquered you, 5
To Byron here where thus I honour you?
The horse that guide the golden eye of heaven,
And blow the morning from their nosterils,
Making their fiery gait above the clouds,
Are not so honoured in their governor, 10
As you, ye slaves, in mighty Tamburlaine.
The headstrong jades of Thrace Alcides tamed,
That King Aegeus fed with human flesh,
And made so wanton that they knew their strengths,
Were not subdued with valour more divine, 15
Than you by this unconquered arm of mine.
To make you fierce, and fit my appetite,
You shall be fed with flesh as raw as blood,
And drink in pails the strongest muscadel:
If you can live with it, then live, and draw 20

94 *masks* lavish entertainment
 s.d. *led by* ed. (led by with O1)
1 *jades* a contemptuous term for a horse
7 *horse* plural
8 *nosterils* nostrils

5 *Asphaltis.* A bituminous lake near Babylon.
6 *Byron.* A city near Babylon.
12 *Alcides.* Hercules. The passage refers to one of his twelve labours.

My chariot swifter than the racking clouds:
If not, then die like beasts, and fit for naught
But perches for the black and fatal ravens.
Thus am I right the scourge of highest Jove,
And see the figure of my dignity,   25
By which I hold my name and majesty.

AMYRAS

Let me have my coach my lord, that I may ride,
And thus be drawn with these two idle kings.

TAMBURLAINE

Thy youth forbids such ease my kingly boy,
They shall tomorrow draw my chariot,   30
While these their fellow kings may be refreshed.

ORCANES

O thou that swayest the region under earth,
And art a king as absolute as Jove,
Come as thou didst in fruitful Sicily,
Surveying all the glories of the land: 35
And as thou took'st the fair Proserpina,
Joying the fruit of Ceres' garden plot,
For love, for honour, and to make her queen,
So for just hate, for shame, and to subdue
This proud contemner of thy dreadful power,   40
Come once in fury and survey his pride,
Haling him headlong to the lowest hell.

THERIDAMAS

Your majesty must get some bits for these,
To bridle their contemptuous cursing tongues,
That like unruly never-broken jades,   45
Break through the hedges of their hateful mouths,
And pass their fixed bounds exceedingly.

TECHELLES

Nay, we will break the hedges of their mouths
And pull their kicking colts out of their pastures.

21 *racking* scudding before the wind
24 *right* indeed
25 *figure* an image of something immaterial
37 *Joying* enjoying   40 *contemner* scorner
46 *hedges . . . mouths* i.e., teeth
49 *their kicking . . . pastures* i.e., their over-active tongues cut out
   of their mouths

---

32 *thou*. Pluto, god of the underworld, who thus carried off the daughter of
Ceres, goddess of the harvest.

USUMCASANE
> Your majesty already hath devised   50
> A mean, as fit as may be to restrain
> These coltish coach-horse tongues from blasphemy.

CELEBINUS
> How like you that sir king? Why speak you not?

KING OF JERUSALEM
> Ah cruel brat, sprung from a tyrant's loins,
> How like his cursed father he begins,   55
> To practise taunts and bitter tyrannies!

TAMBURLAINE
> Ay Turk, I tell thee, this same boy is he,
> That must, advanced in higher pomp than this,
> Rifle the kingdoms I shall leave unsacked,
> If Jove esteeming me too good for earth,   60
> Raise me to match the fair Aldebaran,
> Above the threefold astracism of heaven,
> Before I conquer all the triple world.
> Now fetch me out the Turkish concubines,
> I will prefer them for the funeral   65
> They have bestowed on my abortive son.
>   *The* CONCUBINES *are brought in*
> Where are my common soldiers now, that fought
> So lion-like upon Asphaltis' plains?

SOLDIERS
> Here my lord.

TAMBURLAINE
> Hold ye tall soldiers, take ye queens apiece—   70
> I mean such queens as were kings' concubines.
> Take them, divide them and their jewels too,
> And let them equally serve all your turns.

SOLDIERS
> We thank your majesty.

TAMBURLAINE
> Brawl not, I warn you, for your lechery,   75
> For every man that so offends shall die.

---

62 *threefold astracism* an asterism, or cluster, of three stars
63 *triple world* i.e., composed of Asia, Africa, and Europe
65 *prefer* promote, reward   70 *tall* brave

---

61 *Aldebaran.* A bright star in the constellation of Taurus, one of the
fixed stars of heaven.
70-1 *queens ... queens.* Tamburlaine puns on 'queens' and 'queans'
(whores).

ORCANES
Injurious tyrant, wilt thou so defame
The hateful fortunes of thy victory,
To exercise upon such guiltless dames
The violence of thy common soldiers' lust?   80

TAMBURLAINE
Live continent then, ye slaves, and meet not me
With troops of harlots at your slothful heels.

CONCUBINES
O pity us my lord, and save our honours.

TAMBURLAINE
Are ye not gone ye villains with your spoils?
            The SOLDIERS *run away with the* CONCUBINES

KING OF JERUSALEM
O merciless infernal cruelty!   85

TAMBURLAINE
Save your honours? 'Twere but time indeed
Lost long before you knew what honour meant.

THERIDAMAS
It seems they meant to conquer us my lord,
And make us jesting pageants for their trulls.

TAMBURLAINE
And now themselves shall make our pageant,   90
And common soldiers jest with all their trulls,
Let them take pleasure soundly in their spoils,
Till we prepare our march to Babylon,
Whither we next make expedition.

TECHELLES
Let us not be idle then my lord,   95
But presently be prest to conquer it.

TAMBURLAINE
We will Techelles. Forward then ye jades:
Now crouch ye kings of greatest Asia,
And tremble when ye hear this scourge will come,
That whips down cities, and controlleth crowns,   100
Adding their wealth and treasure to my store.
The Euxine Sea, north to Natolia,

83 s.p. ed. (Lad. O1)
84 s.d. *The* SOLDIERS . . . CONCUBINES ed. (They . . . Ladies O1)
89 *pageants* spectacles
89 *trulls* whores
94 *expedition* haste
96 *presently* quickly
96 *prest* read

The Terrene, west, the Caspian, north-northeast,
And on the south, Sinus Arabicus,
Shall all be loaden with the martial spoils   105
We will convey with us to Persia.
Then shall my native city Samarcanda
And crystal walls of fresh Jaertis' stream,
The pride and beauty of her princely seat,
Be famous through the furthest continents,   110
For there my palace royal shall be placed:
Whose shining turrets shall dismay the heavens,
And cast the fame of Ilion's tower to hell.
Thorough the streets with troop of conquered kings,
I'll ride in golden armour like the sun,   115
And in my helm a triple plume shall spring,
Spangled with diamonds dancing in the air,
To note me emperor of the three-fold world,
Like to an almond tree ymounted high,
Upon the lofty and celestial mount   120
Of ever-green Selinus, quaintly decked
With blooms more white than Erycina's brows,
Whose tender blossoms tremble every one,
At every little breath that thorough heaven is blown:
Then my coach like Saturn's royal son,   125
Mounting his shining chariot, gilt with fire,
And drawn with princely eagles through the path,
Paved with bright crystal, and enchased with stars,
When all the gods stand gazing at his pomp.
So will I ride through Samarcanda streets,   130
Until my soul dissevered from this flesh,

118 *three-fold world* see note to l. 63 above
121 *ever-green* ed. (every greene O1)
126 *chariot* ed. (chariots O1)
128 *enchased* set with

---

104 *Sinus Arabicus.* The Red Sea.
108 *Jaertis' stream.* See note to Part Two, IV, i, 106 above.
113 *Ilion.* Troy.
119–24 *Like . . . blown.* This passage seems to have been borrowed from Spenser's *Faerie Queene*, I, vii, 32, which Marlowe must have seen in manuscript.
121 *Selinus.* A town in Sicily located on a river of the same name.
122 *Erycina.* A name for Venus derived from her temple on Mt Eryx in Sicily.
125 *Saturn's royal son.* i.e., Jove.

Shall mount the milk-white way and meet Him there.
To Babylon my lords, to Babylon!

Exeunt

Act V, Scene i

Enter the GOVERNOR OF BABYLON *upon the walls with* [MAXIMUS *and*] *others*

GOVERNOR OF BABYLON
What saith Maximus?
MAXIMUS
My lord, the breach the enemy hath made
Gives such assurance of our overthrow,
That little hope is left to save our lives,
Or hold our city from the conqueror's hands.   5
Then hang out flags, my lord, of humble truce,
And satisfy the people's general prayers,
That Tamburlaine's intolerable wrath
May be suppressed by our submission.
GOVERNOR OF BABYLON
Villain, respects thou more thy slavish life,   10
Than honour of thy country or thy name?
Is not my life and state as dear to me,
The city and my native country's weal,
As anything of price with thy conceit?
Have we not hope, for all our battered walls,   15
To live secure, and keep his forces out,
When this our famous lake of Limnasphaltis
Makes walls afresh with everything that falls
Into the liquid substance of his stream,
More strong than are the gates of death or hell?   20
What faintness should dismay our courages,
When we are thus defenced against our foe,
And have no terror but his threatening looks?

Enter another [CITIZEN], *kneeling to the* GOVERNOR

s.d. [MAXIMUS *and*] ed. (O1 omits)
14 *As . . . conceit* as anything which may be of value in your thoughts
21 *faintness* weakness
23 s.d. [CITIZEN] ed. (O1 omits)

---

17 *Limnasphaltis.* The bituminous lake of Babylon.

[FIRST CITIZEN]
    My lord, if ever you did deed of ruth,
    And now will work a refuge to our lives,   25
    Offer submission, hang up flags of truce,
    That Tamburlaine may pity our distress,
    And use us like a loving conqueror.
    Though this be held his last day's dreadful siege,
    Wherein he spareth neither man nor child,   30
    Yet are there Christians of Georgia here,
    Whose state he ever pitied and relieved,
    Will get his pardon if your grace would send.
GOVERNOR OF BABYLON
    How is my soul environed,
    And this eternized city of Babylon,   35
    Filled with a pack of faintheart fugitives,
    That thus entreat their shame and servitude?

            [*Enter a second* CITIZEN]

[SECOND CITIZEN]
    My lord, if ever you will win our hearts,
    Yield up the town, save our wives and children:
    For I will cast myself from off these walls,   40
    Or die some death of quickest violence,
    Before I bide the wrath of Tamburlaine.
GOVERNOR OF BABYLON
    Villains, cowards, traitors to our state,
    Fall to the earth, and pierce the pit of hell,
    That legions of tormenting spirits may vex   45
    Your slavish bosoms with continual pains,
    I care not, nor the town will never yield
    As long as any life is in my breast.

        Enter THERIDAMAS *and* TECHELLES, *with other* SOLDIERS

[THERIDAMAS]
    Thou desperate governor of Babylon,
    To save thy life, and us a little labour,   50
    Yield speedily the city to our hands,
    Or else be sure thou shalt be forced with pains,
    More exquisite than ever traitor felt.

    24 s.p. ed. (O1 omits)
    35 *eternized* immortalized
    37 s.d. ed. (O1 omits)
    38 s.p. ed. (O1 omits)

GOVERNOR OF BABYLON
  Tyrant, I turn the traitor in thy throat,
  And will defend it in despite of thee.   55
  Call up the soldiers to defend the walls.
TECHELLES
  Yield foolish governor, we offer more
  Than ever yet we did to such proud slaves,
  As durst resist us till our third day's siege:
  Thou seest us prest to give the last assault,   60
  And that shall bide no more regard of parle.
GOVERNOR OF BABYLON
  Assault and spare not, we will never yield.
           Alarm, and they scale the walls

Enter TAMBURLAINE [*drawn in his chariot by the Kings of* TRE-
BIZON *and* SORIA], *with* USUMCASANE, AMYRAS, *and* CELEBINUS,
with others; the two spare kings [ORCANES, KING OF NATOLIA *and*
JERUSALEM]

TAMBURLAINE
  The stately buildings of fair Babylon,
  Whose lofty pillars, higher than the clouds,
  Were wont to guide the seaman in the deep,   65
  Being carried thither by the cannon's force,
  Now fill the mouth of Limnasphaltis' lake,
  And make a bridge unto the battered walls.
  Where Belus, Ninus, and great Alexander
  Have rode in triumph, triumphs Tamburlaine,   70
  Whose chariot wheels have burst th'Assyrians' bones,
  Drawn with these kings on heaps of carcasses.
  Now in the place where fair Semiramis,
  Courted by kings and peers of Asia,
  Hath trod the measures, do my soldiers march,   75
  And in the streets, where brave Assyrian dames
  Have rid in pomp like rich Saturnia,

60 *prest* ready
62 s.d. [*drawn* . . . SORIA] ed. (O1 omits)
71 *burst* broken
75 *measures* stately dances
76 *brave* finely arrayed, splendid

---

69 *Belus.* Son of Neptune and legendary founder of Babylon. *Ninus.* The
    founder of Nineveh. He married Semiramis, who rebuilt Babylon.
    Alexander. Alexander the Great conquered Babylon in 331 B.C.
77 *Saturnia.* Juno.

With furious words and frowning visages,
My horsemen brandish their unruly blades.

Enter THERIDAMAS *and* TECHELLES, *bringing the* GOVERNOR OF
BABYLON

Who have ye there my lords?   80
THERIDAMAS
The sturdy governor of Babylon,
That made us all the labour for the town,
And used such slender reckoning of your majesty.
TAMBURLAINE
Go bind the villain, he shall hang in chains,
Upon the ruins of this conquered town.   85
Sirrah, the view of our vermillion tents,
Which threatened more than if the region
Next underneath the element of fire,
Were full of comets and of blazing stars,
Whose flaming trains should reach down to the earth   90
Could not affright you; no, nor I myself,
The wrathful messenger of mighty Jove,
That with his sword hath quailed all earthly kings,
Could not persuade you to submission,
But still the ports were shut: villain I say,   95
Should I but touch the rusty gates of hell,
The triple-headed Cerberus would howl,
And wake black Jove to crouch and kneel to me,
But I have sent volleys of shot to you,
Yet could not enter till the breach was made.   100
GOVERNOR OF BABYLON
Nor if my body could have stopped the breach,
Shouldst thou have entered, cruel Tamburlaine:
'Tis not thy bloody tents can make me yield
Nor yet thyself, the anger of the highest,
For though thy cannon shook the city walls,   105
My heart did never quake, nor courage faint.
TAMBURLAINE
Well, now I'll make it quake, go draw him up,

87–8 *region . . . fire* the air
93 *quailed* overpowered
95 *ports* gates

---

97 *Cerberus*. The three-headed dog of hell.
98 *black Jove*. Pluto, ruler of the underworld.

Hang him up in chains upon the city walls,
And let my soldiers shoot the slave to death.

GOVERNOR OF BABYLON

Vile monster, born of some infernal hag,   110
And sent from hell to tyrannize on earth,
Do all thy worst, nor death nor Tamburlaine,
Torture or pain can daunt my dreadless mind.

TAMBURLAINE

Up with him then, his body shall be scarred.

GOVERNOR OF BABYLON

But Tamburlaine, in Limnasphaltis' lake,   115
There lies more gold than Babylon is worth,
Which when the city was besieged I hid,
Save but my life and I will give it thee.

TAMBURLAINE

Then for all your valour, you would save your life.
Whereabout lies it?   120

GOVERNOR OF BABYLON

Under a hollow bank, right opposite
Against the western gate of Babylon.

TAMBURLAINE

Go thither some of you and take his gold.

                     [*Exeunt some* ATTENDANTS]

The rest forward with execution.
Away with him hence, let him speak no more: 125
I think I make your courage something quail.

          [*Exeunt* ATTENDANTS *with* GOVERNOR OF BABYLON]

When this is done we'll march from Babylon,
And make our greatest haste to Persia:
These jades are broken-winded and half tired,
Unharness them, and let me have fresh horse: 130

         [ATTENDANTS *unharness Kings of* TREBIZON *and* SORIA]

So, now their best is done to honour me,
Take them, and hang them both up presently.

KING OF TREBIZON

Vild tyrant, barbarous bloody Tamburlaine!

TAMBURLAINE

Take them away Theridamas, see them dispatched.

123 s.d. ed. (O1 omits)
126 s.d. ed. (O1 omits)
130 s.d. ed. (O1 omits)
132 *presently* immediately
133 *Vild* vile

THERIDAMAS
     I will my lord.   135
          [*Exit* THERIDAMAS *with the Kings of* TREBIZON *and* SORIA]
TAMBURLAINE
     Come Asian viceroys, to your tasks a while
     And take such fortune as your fellows felt.
ORCANES
     First let thy Scythian horse tear both our limbs
     Rather than we should draw thy chariot,
     And like base slaves abject our princely minds   140
     To vile and ignominious servitude.
KING OF JERUSALEM
     Rather lend me thy weapon Tamburlaine,
     That I may sheathe it in this breast of mine.
     A thousand deaths could not torment our hearts
     More than the thought of this doth vex our souls.   145
AMYRAS
     They will talk still my lord, if you do not bridle them.
TAMBURLAINE
     Bridle them and let me to my coach.

They bridle them. [*The* GOVERNOR OF BABYLON *appears hanging*
          in chains on the walls. Enter THERIDAMAS]

AMYRAS
     See now my lord how brave the captain hangs.
TAMBURLAINE
     'Tis brave indeed my boy, well done,
     Shoot first my lord, and then the rest shall follow.   150
THERIDAMAS
     Then have at him to begin withal.
                                             THERIDAMAS *shoots*
GOVERNOR OF BABYLON
     Yet save my life and let this wound appease
     The mortal fury of great Tamburlaine.
TAMBURLAINE
     No, though Asphaltis' lake were liquid gold,
     And offered me as ransom for thy life,   155
     Yet shouldst thou die, shoot at him all at once.
                                             They shoot

135 s.d. ed. (O1 omits)
137 *take . . . felt* share the fate of your fellow kings
140 *abject* abase
147 s.d. [*The . . .* THERIDAMAS] ed. (O1 omits)   148 *brave* excellently
151 *have . . . withal* I shall attack him, for a start

So now he hangs like Bagdet's governor,
Having as many bullets in his flesh,
As there be breaches in her battered wall.
Go now and bind the burghers hand and foot,   160
And cast them headlong in the city's lake:
Tartars and Persians shall inhabit there,
And to command the city, I will build
A citadel, that all Africa
Which hath been subject to the Persian king,   165
Shall pay me tribute for, in Babylon.

TECHELLES
What shall be done with their wives and children my lord?

TAMBURLAINE
Techelles, drown them all, man, woman, and child,
Leave not a Babylonian in the town.

TECHELLES
I will about it straight, come soldiers.   *Exit*   170

TAMBURLAINE
Now Casane, where's the Turkish Alcoran,
And all the heaps of superstitious books,
Found in the temples of that Mahomet,
Whom I have thought god? They shall be burnt.

USUMCASANE
Here they are my lord.   175

TAMBURLAINE
Well said, let there be a fire presently.

                                   [*They light a fire*]
In vain, I see, men worship Mahomet.
My sword hath sent millions of Turks to hell,
Slew all his priests, his kinsmen, and his friends,
And yet I live untouched by Mahomet: 180
There is a God full of revenging wrath,
From whom the thunder and the lightning breaks,
Whose scourge I am, and Him will I obey.
So Casane, fling them in the fire.

                                   [*They burn the books*]
Now Mahomet, if thou have any power,   185
Come down thyself and work a miracle,
Thou art not worthy to be worshipped,
That suffers flames of fire to burn the writ

157 *Bagdet's* Bagdad's
176 s.d. ed. (O1 omits)
184 s.d. ed. (O1 omits)

Wherein the sum of thy religion rests.
Why send'st thou not a furious whirlwind down,   190
To blow thy Alcoran up to thy throne,
Where men report thou sitt'st by God Himself,
Or vengeance on the head of Tamburlaine,
That shakes his sword against thy majesty,
And spurns the abstracts of thy foolish laws?   195
Well soldiers, Mahomet remains in hell,
He cannot hear the voice of Tamburlaine.
Seek out another godhead to adore,
The God that sits in heaven, if any god,
For he is God alone, and none but He.   200

[*Enter* TECHELLES]

TECHELLES
I have fulfilled your highness' will, my lord,
Thousands of men drowned in Asphaltis' lake,
Have made the water swell above the banks,
And fishes fed by human carcasses,
Amazed, swim up and down upon the waves,   205
As when they swallow asafoetida,
Which makes them fleet aloft and gasp for air.
TAMBURLAINE
Well then my friendly lords, what now remains
But that we leave sufficient garrison
And presently depart to Persia,   210
To triumph after all our victories.
THERIDAMAS
Ay, good my lord, let us in haste to Persia,
And let this captain be removed the walls,
To some high hill about the city here.
TAMBURLAINE
Let it be so, about it soldiers: 215
But stay, I feel myself distempered suddenly.
TECHELLES
What is it dares distemper Tamburlaine?
TAMBURLAINE
Something Techelles, but I know not what,
But forth ye vassals, whatso'er it be,
Sickness or death can never cónquer me.   *Exeunt*   220

200 s.d. ed. (O1 omits)   204 *fed* ed. (fied O1)
206 *asafoetida* a concreted resinous gum with a strong odour, used in
    cooking and medicine
207 *fleet* float   216 *distempered* sick, ailing, disordered

Act V, Scene ii

Enter CALLAPINE, KING OF AMASIA, [CAPTAIN,] *with drums and trumpets*

CALLAPINE

    King of Amasia, now our mighty host,
    Marcheth in Asia Major, where the streams
    Of Euphrates and Tigris swiftly runs,
    And here may we behold great Babylon,
    Circled about with Limnasphaltis' lake,   5
    Where Tamburlaine with all his army lies,
    Which being faint and weary with the siege,
    We may lie ready to encounter him,
    Before his host be full from Babylon,
    And so revenge our latest grievous loss,   10
    If God or Mahomet send any aid.

KING OF AMASIA

    Doubt not my lord, but we shall conquer him.
    The monster that hath drunk a sea of blood,
    And yet gapes still for more to quench his thirst,
    Our Turkish swords shall headlong send to hell,   15
    And that vile carcass drawn by warlike kings,
    The fowls shall eat, for never sepulchre
    Shall grace the base-born tyrant Tamburlaine.

CALLAPINE

    When I record my parents' slavish life,
    Their cruel death, mine own captivity,   20
    My viceroys' bondage under Tamburlaine,
    Methinks I could sustain a thousand deaths,
    To be revenged of all his villainy.
    Ah sacred Mahomet, thou that hast seen
    Millions of Turks perish by Tamburlaine,   25
    Kingdoms made waste, brave cities sacked and burnt,
    And but one host is left to honour thee:
    Aid thy obedient servant Callapine,
    And make him after all these overthrows,
    To triumph over cursed Tamburlaine.   30

KING OF AMASIA

    Fear not my lord, I see great Mahomet
    Clothed in purple clouds, and on his head
    A chaplet brighter than Apollo's crown,

s.d. [CAPTAIN,] ed. (O1 omits)   19 *record* call to mind

Marching about the air with armed men,
To join with you against this Tamburlaine.   35
[CAPTAIN]
Renowned general, mighty Callapine,
Though God himself and holy Mahomet
Should come in person to resist your power,
Yet might your mighty host encounter all,
And pull proud Tamburlaine upon his knees,   40
To sue for mercy at your highness' feet.
CALLAPINE
Captain, the force of Tamburlaine is great,
His fortune greater, and the victories
Wherewith he hath so sore dismayed the world,
Are greatest to discourage all our drifts;   45
Yet when the pride of Cynthia is at full,
She wanes again, and so shall his I hope,
For we have here the chief selected men
Of twenty several kingdoms at the least:
Nor plowman, priest, nor merchant stays at home,   50
All Turkey is in arms with Callapine,
And never will we sunder camps and arms,
Before himself or his be conquered.
This is the time that must eternize me,
For conquering the tyrant of the world.   55
Come soldiers, let us lie in wait for him
And if we find him absent from his camp,
Or that it be rejoined again at full,
Assail it and be sure of victory.   *Exeunt*

Act V, Scene iii

[*Enter*] THERIDAMAS, TECHELLES, USUMCASANE

[THERIDAMAS]
Weep heavens, and vanish into liquid tears,
Fall stars that govern his nativity,
And summon all the shining lamps of heaven
To cast their bootless fires to the earth,

36 s.p. ed. (O1 omits)   45 *drifts* purposes
49 *several* different
54 *eternize* immortalize
58 *Or that* before
 1 s.p. ed. (O1 omits)
 4 *bootless* unavailing

And shed their feeble influence in the air.   5
Muffle your beauties with eternal clouds,
For hell and darkness pitch their pitchy tents,
And death with armies of Cimmerian spirits
Gives battle 'gainst the heart of Tamburlaine.
Now in defiance of that wonted love,   10
Your sacred virtues poured upon his throne,
And made his state an honour to the heavens,
These cowards invisible assail his soul,
And threaten conquest on our sovereign:
But if he die, your glories are disgraced,   15
Earth droops and says, that hell in heaven is placed.

TECHELLES
O then ye powers that sway eternal seats,
And guide this massy substance of the earth,
If you retain desert of holiness,
As your supreme estates instruct our thoughts,   20
Be not inconstant, careless of your fame,
Bear not the burden of your enemies' joys,
Triumphing in his fall whom you advanced,
But as his birth, life, health and majesty
Were strangely blessed and governed by heaven,   25
So honour heaven till heaven dissolved be,
His birth, his life, his health and majesty.

USUMCASANE
Blush heaven to lose the honour of thy name,
To see thy footstool set upon thy head,
And let no baseness in thy haughty breast,   30
Sustain a shame of such inexcellence:
To see the devils mount in angels' thrones,
And angels dive into the pools of hell.
And though they think their painful date is out,
And that their power is puissant as Jove's,   35
Which makes them manage arms against thy state,
Yet make them feel the strength of Tamburlaine,
Thy instrument and note of majesty,

19 *desert of holiness* that which deserves religious worship
20 *estates* ranks, authorities
22 *Bear . . . burden* do not join in the chorus; *burden* ed. (burthen
     O1)
31 *Sustain . . . inexcellence* bear so vile a shame
38 *note* distinguishing mark

---

8 *Cimmerian.* Dark, infernal. See note in Part One, III, ii, 77 above.

Is greater far than they can thus subdue,
For if he die, thy glory is disgraced,   40
Earth droops and says that hell in heaven is placed.

[Enter TAMBURLAINE, *drawn in his chariot by the captive kings,*
ORCANES *and* JERUSALEM; AMYRAS, CELEBINUS, *and* PHYSICIANS]

TAMBURLAINE
What daring god torments my body thus
And seeks to conquer mighty Tamburlaine?
Shall sickness prove me now to be a man,
That have been termed the terror of the world?   45
Techelles and the rest, come take your swords,
And threaten him whose hand afflicts my soul,
Come let us march against the powers of heaven,
And set black streamers in the firmament,
To signify the slaughter of the gods.   50
Ah friends, what shall I do? I cannot stand,
Come carry me to war against the gods,
That thus envy the health of Tamburlaine.
THERIDAMAS
Ah good my lord, leave these impatient words,
Which add much danger to your malady.   55
TAMBURLAINE
Why shall I sit and languish in this pain?
No, strike the drums, and in revenge of this,
Come let us charge our spears and pierce his breast,
Whose shoulders bear the axis of the world,
That if I perish, heaven and earth may fade.   60
Theridamas, haste to the court of Jove,
Will him to send Apollo hither straight,
To cure me, or I'll fetch him down myself.
TECHELLES
Sit still my gracious lord, this grief will cease,
And cannot last, it is so violent.   65
TAMBURLAINE
Not last Techelles? No, for I shall die.
See where my slave, the ugly monster Death

41 s.d. ed. (O1 omits)
49 *streamers* pennons
58 *charge* level
62 *Apollo* the god of medicine
64 *grief* pain

58–9 *his . . . world.* Atlas' breast. He bore the heavens, not the earth.

Shaking and quivering, pale and wan for fear,
Stands aiming at me with his murdering dart,
Who flies away at every glance I give,   70
And when I look away, comes stealing on:
Villain away, and hie thee to the field,
I and mine army come to load thy bark
With souls of thousand mangled carcasses.
Look where he goes, but see, he comes again   75
Because I stay. Techelles let us march,
And weary Death with bearing souls to hell.

PHYSICIAN
Pleaseth your majesty to drink this potion,
Which will abate the fury of your fit,
And cause some milder spirits govern you.   80

TAMBURLAINE
Tell me, what think you of my sickness now?

PHYSICIAN
I viewed your urine and the hypostasis
Thick and obscure doth make your danger great,
Your veins are full of accidental heat,
Whereby the moisture of your blood is dried,   85
The humidum and calor, which some hold
Is not a parcel of the elements,
But of a substance more divine and pure,
Is almost clean extinguished and spent,
Which being the cause of life imports your death.   90
Besides my lord, this day is critical,

---

69 *murdering* ed. (murthering O1)   76 *stay* delay
82 *hypostasis* accumulation of solids within a fluid; sediment
84 *accidental* abnormal; in excess of the proper amount
86 *humidum and calor* moisture and heat, which in combination form
   the sanguine humour
87 *parcel* part
91 *day is critical* i.e., the stars are in an unfavourable conjunction
   for effecting a cure

78-99 *Pleaseth . . . all.* 'As a result of his intense passion (and . . . as a
   result of the position of his stars), Tamburlaine has occasioned in his
   body an excess of febrile heat. This "accidental heat" parches his
   arteries and dried up in his blood the radical moisture (*humidum*) which
   is necessary for the preservation of his natural heat (*calor*). The deple-
   tion of his *humidum* and *calor* (whose admixture in the blood gives rise
   to the *spirits*) prevents his soul's functions, stops his bodily activities,
   and thereby causes his death.' (Johnstone Parr, *Tamburlaine's Malady*
   . . ., p. 19.)

Dangerous to those whose crisis is as yours:
Your artiers which alongst the veins convey
The lively spirits which the heart engenders
Are parched and void of spirit, that the soul   95
Wanting those organons by which it moves,
Cannot endure by argument of art.
Yet if your majesty may escape this day,
No doubt but you may soon recover all.

TAMBURLAINE
Then will I comfort all my vital parts,   100
And live in spite of death above a day.

Alarm within. [*Enter a* MESSENGER]

MESSENGER
My lord, young Callapine that lately fled from your majesty,
hath now gathered a fresh army, and hearing your absence in
the field, offers to set upon us presently.

TAMBURLAINE
See my physicians now, how Jove hath sent   105
A present medicine to recure my pain:
My looks shall make them fly, and might I follow,
There should not one of all the villain's power
Live to give offer of another fight.

USUMCASANE
I joy my lord, your highness is so strong,   110
That can endure so well your royal presence,
Which only will dismay the enemy.

TAMBURLAINE
I know it will Casane: draw you slaves,
In spite of death I will go show my face.

Alarm. TAMBURLAINE *goes in and comes out again with all the rest*

Thus are the villains, cowards fled for fear,   115
Like summer's vapours, vanished by the sun,
And could I but a while pursue the field,
That Callapine should be my slave again.
But I perceive my martial strength is spent,
In vain I strive and rail against those powers   120

93 *artiers* arteries
96 *organons* organs of the body which act as instruments of the soul
101 s.d. [*Enter a* MESSENGER] ed. (O1 omits)
104 *presently* immediately   106 *recure* cure
111 *That . . . well* I who find so much pleasure in
112 *only* alone

That mean t'invest me in a higher throne,
As much too high for this disdainful earth.
Give me a map, then let me see how much
Is left for me to conquer all the world,
That these my boys may finish all my wants.　　　125

One brings a map

Here I began to march toward Persia,
Along Armenia and the Caspian Sea,
And thence into Bithynia, where I took
The Turk and his great empress prisoners,
Then marched I into Egypt and Arabia,　　　130
And here not far from Alexandria,
Whereas the Terrene and the Red Sea meet,
Being distant less than full a hundred leagues,
I meant to cut a channel to them both,
That men might quickly sail to India.　　　135
From thence to Nubia near Borno lake,
And so along the Ethiopian sea,
Cutting the tropic line of Capricorn,
I conquered all as far as Zanzibar.
Then by the northern part of Africa,　　　140
I came at last to Graecia, and from thence
To Asia, where I stay against my will,
Which is from Scythia, where I first began,
Backward and forwards near five thousand leagues.
Look here my boys, see what a world of ground　　　145
Lies westward from the midst of Cancer's line,
Unto the rising of this earthly globe,
Whereas the sun declining from our sight,
Begins the day with our antipodes:
And shall I die and this unconquered?　　　150
Lo here my sons, are all the golden mines,
Inestimable drugs and precious stones,
More worth than Asia, and the world beside,
And from th'Antartique Pole, eastward behold

---

132 *Whereas* where

---

134 *cut a channel.* Make a canal. The Suez Canal had been suggested before
　　Marlowe's day.
146 *the midst of Cancer's line.* Just off the coast of north-west Africa where,
　　according to Ortelius, the meridian O° intersects the Tropic of Cancer.
149 *antipodes.* See note to Part Two, I, iii, 52 above.
154–5 *And from ... descried.* Australia, which had not yet been 'descried'
　　(discovered) but about which rumours were current.

As much more land, which never was descried,   155
Wherein are rocks of pearl, that shine as bright
As all the lamps that beautify the sky,
And shall I die, and this unconquered?
Here lovely boys, what death forbids my life,
That let your lives command in spite of death.   160

AMYRAS

Alas my lord, how should our bleeding hearts
Wounded and broken with your highness' grief,
Retain a thought of joy, or spark of life?
Your soul gives essence to our wretched subjects,
Whose matter is incorporate in your flesh.   165

CELEBINUS

Your pains do pierce our souls, no hope survives,
For by your life we entertain our lives.

TAMBURLAINE

But sons, this subject not of force enough,
To hold the fiery spirit it contains,
Must part, imparting his impressions,   170
By equal portions into both your breasts:
My flesh divided in your precious shapes,
Shall still retain my spirit, though I die,
And live in all your souls immortally:
Then now remove me, that I may resign   175
My place and proper title to my son:
First take my scourge and my imperial crown,
And mount my royal chariot of estate,
That I may see thee crowned before I die.
Help me, my lords, to make my last remove.   180
          [*They help* TAMBURLAINE *out of his chariot*]

THERIDAMAS

A woeful change my lord, that daunts our thoughts,
More than the ruin of our proper souls.

TAMBURLAINE

Sit up my son, let me see how well
Thou wilt become thy father's majesty.
          They crown [AMYRAS]

162 *grief* suffering   167 *entertain* maintain
168 *subject* material body   170 *his impressions* its spiritual power
176 *proper* own   184 s.d. [AMYRAS] ed. (him O1)

164–5 *Your soul . . . flesh.* Your soul has bequeathed an animating spirit
     (essence) to our material bodies (subjects), since our bodies are part of
     your flesh.

AMYRAS
  With what a flinty bosom should I joy   185
  The breath of life, and burden of my soul,
  If not resolved into resolved pains,
  My body's mortified lineaments
  Should exercise the motions of my heart,
  Pierced with the joy of any dignity!   190
  O father, if the unrelenting ears
  Of death and hell be shut against my prayers,
  And that the spiteful influence of heaven
  Deny my soul fruition of her joy,
  How should I step or stir my hateful feet,   195
  Against the inward powers of my heart,
  Leading a life that only strives to die,
  And plead in vain, unpleasing sovereignty?

TAMBURLAINE
  Let not thy love exceed thine honour son,
  Nor bar thy mind that magnanimity,   200
  That nobly must admit necessity:
  Sit up my boy, and with those silken reins,
  Bridle the steeled stomachs of those jades.

THERIDAMAS
  My lord, you must obey his majesty,
  Since fate commands and proud necessity.   205

AMYRAS
  Heavens witness me, with what a broken heart
  And damned spirit I ascend this seat,
  And send my soul before my father die,
  His anguish and his burning agony.

TAMBURLAINE
  Now fetch the hearse of fair Zenocrate,   210
  Let it be placed by this my fatal chair,
  And serve as parcel of my funeral.

---

186 *burden* ed. (burthen O1)   200 *magnanimity* fortitude
203 *steeled stomachs* obdurately proud spirits
212 *parcel* part

185–90 *With . . . dignity.* 'How hard a heart I should have if I could enjoy
    my life and the possession of my soul and if my body were not dissolved
    in extreme pain [l. 187] and sympathetically afflicted [l. 188] and could
    still direct the movements of a heart that was touched to joy by such
    things as earthly dignities' (Ellis-Fermor).
208 *send.* May the heavens send. Amyras wants to share in his father's
    death-agony.

USUMCASANE
Then feels your majesty no sovereign ease,
Nor may our hearts all drowned in tears of blood,
Joy any hope of your recovery?   215
TAMBURLAINE
Casane no, the monarch of the earth,
And eyeless monster that torments my soul,
Cannot behold the tears ye shed for me,
And therefore still augments his cruelty.
TECHELLES
Then let some god oppose his holy power,   220
Against the wrath and tyranny of death,
That his tear-thirsty and unquenched hate
May be upon himself reverberate.
                    They bring in the hearse [*of* ZENOCRATE]
TAMBURLAINE
Now eyes, enjoy your latest benefit,
And when my soul hath virtue of your sight,   225
Pierce through the coffin and the sheet of gold,
And glut your longings with a heaven of joy.
So, reign my son, scourge and control these slaves,
Guiding thy chariot with thy father's hand.
As precious is the charge thou undertak'st   230
As that which Clymene's brain-sick son did guide,
When wandering Phoebe's ivory cheeks were scorched
And all the earth like Aetna breathing fire:
Be warned by him, then learn with awful eye
To sway a throne as dangerous as his: 235
For if thy body thrive not full of thoughts
As pure and fiery as Phyteus' beams,
The nature of these proud revelling jades
Will take occasion by the slenderest hair,

215 *Joy* enjoy
223 s.d. [*of* ZENOCRATE] ed. (O1 omits)
231 *Clymene's* O2 (Clymeus O1)
232 *Phoebe* the moon
234 *awful* awe-inspiring
237 *Phyteus* Pythius, another name for Apollo, the sun-god
238 *these . . . jades* the conquered kings

225 *when . . . sight.* When (after death) my soul will have the power of vision
   which in life belongs only to the eyes.
231 *Clymene's . . . son.* See note to Part One, IV, ii, 49 above.

And draw thee piecemeal like Hippolytus,　　　　　240
Through rocks more steep and sharp than Caspian clifts.
The nature of thy chariot will not bear
A guide of lesser temper than myself,
More than heaven's coach the pride of Phaëton.
Farewell my boys, my dearest friends, farewell,　　　　　245
My body feels, my soul doth weep to see
Your sweet desires deprived my company,
For Tamburlaine, the Scourge of God must die.

　　　　　　　　　　　　　　　　　[Dies]

AMYRAS
Meet heaven and earth, and here let all things end,
For earth hath spent the pride of all her fruit,　　　　　250
And heaven consumed his choicest living fire.
Let earth and heaven his timeless death deplore,
For both their worths can equal him no more.

　　　　　　　　　　　　　　　　　[Exeunt]

241 *clifts* cliffs
248 s.d. ed. (O1 omits)
252 *timeless* untimely
253 s.d. ed. (O1 omits)

---

240 *Hippolytus.* Killed when his horses, frightened by the god Poseidon,
bolted and dragged him to death.
244 *Phaëton.* See note to Part One, IV, ii, 49 above.